EXPERIENCES EXPRESSED

DIRECT FROM THE CORE

RITESH BHATIA

Maa

I am because of you.

Contents

Contents

Contents

FOREWORD

In *Experiences Expressed* **Ritesh Bhatia** shares his unique, innocent, and authentic insights on a wide range of every-day life events, issues, and habits, that most of us, including me, overlook, ignore, or are just too focused on our habitual busy-ness.

Take 4 minutes to open this treasure chest to one of his invitations to see or ponder what you have overlooked for a lifetime. It is very likely to improve the color or mood of your day. Think of this 4-minute daily retreat for your brain as a vacation away from your same-old, same-old hectic life.

In reading several of these Experiences, they made me think a little bit differently, from a different perspective, I wondered . . . is this my experience? – Yes, in some cases. Not exactly, in some cases. And either way, the experience gave me the great gift of time to pause, reflect, celebrate, and reconsider, all of which enriched me in less than 4 minutes! How many things in your life can you say that about?

Ritesh taps into the innate human inquisitiveness of:

- Who am I?
- What am I here for?
- How am I going about my life?
- Is there more to life?
- What am I missing?
- What do I have to celebrate, and be grateful for?

In my experience, to change anything about how I think, what I do, or the attitudes and beliefs that guide my decisions and actions have begun with raising my level of awareness about myself. The concept of myself includes several concepts of "self". I have a physical self. I have a cultural self. I have an educated self. I have a career(s) self. I have a Core SELF. Well, you get the idea.

What I love about this collection of Ritesh's *Experiences Expressed* is helping to raise the reader's awareness about multiple aspects of one's life. Like Ralph Waldo Emerson said, "The mind, once stretched by a new idea, never returns to its original dimensions."

Some of the stories have the potential to raise awareness in one portion of your life, other stories may affect your life's journey. In any case, each shared experience is a treasure for you to ponder how it pertains to you, your life, and your life's journey.

The bottom line, you are the only person who is responsible for your own life. So sit back with your favorite, time-of-day-appropriate beverage and read about one or more of Ritesh's *Experiences Expressed* that will surely raise your own level of awareness about how you are doing your life now . . . and maybe even open up the opportunity to improve on it!

Peter J. Reding

Author of *Positively Brilliant Self-mastery – Reclaim Your Authentic Self Now*

Founder, www.CoreSELFie.com

PREFACE

Like any other ordinary person, I know exactly how a human brain looks. I also know how to draw a well-labeled diagram of my heart in notebooks. However, one thing that intrigues me the most is the human-construed phenomenon called the mind. If I have to give my mind a shape, a design, a color — what can it be?

After careful deliberation, I have come to the conclusion that maybe the human mind is designed as an enormous library with multiple shelves stacked with experiences. Each experience originates from the stories of our own lives and from the lives of others: experiences we cherish, experiences we use as reference, and experiences that help us make sense of the world around us.

At the center of all these experiences is our core. There exists in each one of us an uninhibited inner place that is formless and boundaryless — that some of us refer to as 'our core' while that the others attribute as 'our source' or 'a higher power'. Irrespective of what we may name it and how we may describe it, this place becomes our personal monastery that can offer us the blueprint of our own life's purpose.

Through my first ever book, **Experiences Expressed**, it is your personal monastery that I want to speak to. It is the rich layer of the shelves of your experiences that I want to add to.

Experiences Expressed is my endeavor to establish a dialogue between your core and mine. It is an endeavor to share heartfelt experiences from my personal life as well as my coaching practice with you so that the life-affirming ideas of happiness, love, contentment, peace, and fulfillment can gain as much momentum as possible to grow and expand!

For ease of reading, I have structured this book around five contemporary themes — Dialogue with Life, The 'We' in 'Me', Face to Face with Emotions, Diving Within, and The Case of Values. Each anecdote within these themes will hopefully open up a world of possibilities, introspection, and deeper living for you.

The book is based on two beliefs of mine:

What we give attention to gains power and expands: I hope the tireless work that I have done to reinforce life-affirming ideas in this book will gain energy in your life and manifest in your existence!

We can learn immensely from experiences — not just ours but also those of others: I hope my experiences will add to the richness and eternal wisdom of your life.

And as I read somewhere, write — not because you have the right words to present in tidy paragraphs, but because you have noticed life and have a love offering to make to your world! Experiences Expressed is my love offering to this universe and to every beautiful being that forms a part of it.

Happy Reading!

Acknowledgements

A heart filled with gratitude, and words so few to ever be adequate enough:

To my **BABA**, who has always been giving me more than I ever thought I deserved.

To my **Mom**, whose unwavering support is my source of strength.

To **Deepa**, whose support made it possible for me to align my work with my life purpose.

To **Kishneet**, without whom this book would have not taken the shape it finally took.

To my mentors, **Peter** and **Leon**, whose wisdom has been my guiding light in this work.

To my **clients**, whose experiences have added to the richness of my life.

To my **friends**, whose acknowledgments became a source of motivation for me.

To my **family members**, who have always wished me well.

And last, but not the least, thank you to all the **readers** who have decided to give this book a part of their time.

ONENESS

RITESH BHATIA

Dialogue with Life

I

Taking a Back Seat

Some of the greatest teachers of all times across cultures have urged us to be mindful; mindful of every act that we get into. But one of the most ignored aspects of mindfulness is to be fully awake and responsive to the pause, the halt between one movement and the other – to be mindful enough to differentiate one step from the other; to be mindful enough of the spaces that we give between words. This was one of the realizations that came my way when I decided to take a cab against my usual instinct and habit of driving myself.

What I thought would be an ordinary change in my natural routine surprisingly turned out to be the most pleasing start to my day. Unplanned blessings sometimes come in the form of a decision to take a backseat. At least, so it was in my case.

As I made myself comfortable in the car taking a pause from driving, I was thrilled to see how the same path that I was so familiar with had begun to take a life of its own. What normally appears to the one driving as patches of green were unfolding themselves as beautiful plants and flowers! What normally appears to the one driving as patches of brown and black were unfolding themselves as roads with mesmerizing forks and curves! I could afford to notice the serenity of the deities in the temples that passed by.

All this made me come to a realization that often when we place ourselves in the driving seat of our lives – taking charge of the speed and direction in which we want it to lead - we begin to be nervous about not letting our foot off the pedal. The mere thought of not being in control (behind that steering wheel) makes us think that our life will come to a halt and things will stop moving.

But what I experienced that day was a revelation for me: the fact that our journeys do not stop even when we take a backseat. Though that day my journey might not have been at the same speed and manner in which it would have been if I was self-driving, what I could gain in exchange of that was a whole new experience, a whole new perspective, and also a completely different rendezvous with so many things that I was usually missing while I was acting the lead.

The sight of the passing tea shops, which I never noticed earlier, made me realize that though the destination was important I could have accumulated so many more memories and moments if only I would have stopped by at one of those, and still would have reached where I intended to in a much more fun and fulfilling way.

And as if all this was not enough of a gift for me, mid-way I also noticed a signboard showing a shorter and much smoother route to the same destination. My thoughts – I got so familiar and comfortable with taking the normal yet longer route that I was unaware of the newer and much easier way of getting to the same place that I intended to. In life, we must slow down and take a back seat at times, which also has a chance of bringing up an alternate way that in fact can take us to the same place that we intend to go, while we relax and lower our speed and at the same time accumulate a bunch of new experiences.

To top it all, simply priceless was receiving the joy and liberty of taking that moment to close my eyes while the car was still moving and reflect that all this would not have been possible in the middle of the act of driving but only when I decided to take a pause from it.

While the cab stopped at my destination and I had to clear the bill, I shut my eyes for a final few minutes to embrace myself with the reflections that consumed me as a consequence of a very enriching ride. The following thoughts sprung up like fireworks in my mind:

Once we begin a journey, we are most likely bound to reach the destination we may have chosen. But by occasionally taking a back seat, observing the splendor around, disengaging from actions, and being reflective ensures that we build awareness of the roads that we are taking, the impact they are having on us, and be better prepared for our destination.

The ebb and flow of life are such that it will continue to throb and move irrespective of our participation in it. However, how aware we are of this movement and how mindfully are we able to enjoy it is determined by our ability to sit back and introspect.

There goes a Zen saying that we cannot see our reflection in running water. It is only in the still water that we can see. Rightly so, in the hustle of our daily lives we can never find the fullness which a moment of silent introspection can bless us with.

How aware we are of this movement and how mindfully are we able to enjoy it is determined by our ability to sit back and introspect.

II

Slow Down

Among the greatest things to be found,
the being of nothingness is by far the greatest.
~ Leonardo Da Vinci

When I was first initiated into the process of nothingness and the practice called Slowing Down, I remember having spent almost an entire week doing absolutely nothing.

As you would have guessed by the name, the process and practice of slowing down revolve around the pace of things in life. It is about being able to relish the present and give it all the attention it deserves. It is about not living life as if it needed to be rushed from one moment to another to reach somewhere. It is about savouring each and every flavour life has to offer to the fullest as if we have all the time in the world. It is about matching and syncing our speed, our breaths to the pace of our natural self and to that of the rhythm of life.

Slowing down! How simple this phrase sounds, right?

The immediate picture that had formed in my mind was that of someone applying the brakes. It was of me becoming someone from whom there is nothing that is demanded to be done.

In fact, my assumption had been that the maximum this process might demand from me is doing less and doing it slowly. And how difficult that can be! Well, I can say from experience now that it is not that simple.

I had conveniently assumed that it takes no effort to practise this thing called slowing down, and all that I will have to do is pick up fewer tasks in my routine.

I had felt that the only thing it can demand from me is that I may have to be mindful of not rushing into things. It sounded so easy. Simple is what I thought of it to be.

And then the initiation and the week of nil activity happened and I realised it was a real roller-coaster ride – Not being able to take a simple pause, not being able to find a way to match my rhythm to the rhythm of life.

A moment of success and then hours and hours of not being able to practice the so-called simple practice of slowing down had made me understand its essence and what it really meant.

The process and practice also helped me realise what I had created out of this beautiful life that I had got. It made me come to a conclusion that regardless of whatever blessing I think of my life to be, there is yet so much that I had still eluded myself of.

And it is all this that made me promise to myself that I will continue this journey of slowing down until I am able to give myself this art and habit of being in the zone of nothingness whenever I want to. And my journey is still continuing.

As I share my experience candidly with this process of nothingness and the practice of slowing down, I also invite you to take a chance to reflect on the pace at which you are living your life.

Irrespective of whether you are happy about it or not, see if you actually can slow down. Are you able to reduce the pace at which you are living your life?

However, as you venture into this world, just a word of caution! Do not mistake slowing down with not doing your office work and instead sitting down to watch a movie. Or do not confuse it with not socialising with friends, and instead spending your time at home with your family or yourself.

Slowing down is not about breaking free from your regular chores in the kitchen and instead reading a book. It is not assuming that gardening is any better than running on the treadmill and burning some calories.

Now that I have nudged you in the direction of what slowing down is not, I hope you are able to spend some time in figuring out what slowing down means to you.

I hope you are able to experience it in your own unique way. And trust me when I say this, the act of slowing down has the potential of becoming the biggest gift that you could offer to yourself.

Regardless of whatever blessing I think of my life to be, there is yet so much that I had still eluded myself of.

III

Slowwwww

If you are always racing to the next moment,
what happens to the one you are in?
~ Nanette Mathews

While you will hardly find people who would object to the practice of slowing down in principle, almost all of us struggle to adopt this as a habit in our lives. Despite the immense impact that slowing down can trigger in our experiences, its adoption in our lives is almost every time accompanied by difficulties.

Having practiced this act myself and having received its advantages in abundance, I want to use this space to share a couple of practices where slowing down can be experienced by anyone who is interested.

These practices will surely not come easy, but no matter how many times one fails with them, even the mere act of trying them will show how magnificent the habit of slowing down would be if adopted.

Before I get into sharing the two practices, I would like to mention the potential barriers to slowing down. I am mentioning them first because they will show themselves first, much before you take your first step towards slowing down in your life.

These barriers majorly come in the form of apprehensions and doubts. Apprehensions are not only about one's ability to be able to slow down, but also about being doubtful about losing on things that are perceived as important to hold on to or achieve.

Well, I call these thoughts apprehensions, as I have experienced them myself, and have also seen how invalid they are. I have myself gone through thinking about how I will be able to manage all my daily tasks and commitments if I slow down in life. What all will I have to let go of once I adopt slowing down as a practice in my life? And then the final supreme question: when things are supposed to be achieved by doing, and not by not doing, how am I supposed to benefit by embracing slowing down?

I have shared some examples of the kind of questions that may arise. But there can be many more different and seemingly bigger ones that may come up for you. My suggestion? LET THEM COME AND GO!

And once you have been through a phase of QnA, you can start practicing slowing down in the areas of your life that you feel can easily allow the flow of this process and practice.

I am now going to share the two areas in which I implemented this, but they are just for reference. And I would say, you must think through and decide what works best for you.

The first practice where I adopted slowing down in my life is in the speed at which I speak. I realized that this was one thing connected to me, where not only me but a rush has been experienced by many who know me.

So instead of choosing anything which may be easier, I decided to slow down my pace of speaking. And yes, I keep failing in it almost every day, but at least now I know what difference I find in my thoughts and my heartbeats, whenever I can consciously slow down my speed of speech.

It has made my conversations much more soothing, a lot more sensitive, and has made them more meaningful too. This practice of slowing down my pace of speech has made me much happier with what I speak now because it's both me and the ones who are listening, who seem to better connect with the conversation that is taking place.

The second practice is slowing down my speed of replying to text messages or emails that I get. Though I did not anticipate any big changes to happen, I adopted this as a part of the bigger package of slowing down in most areas of my life. But the effects that I have experienced surprised me too.

I have seen a difference in the kind of responses I am sending now. Not only is the message exactly as I wanted it to be (so no second thoughts later), I see my responses as much more affectionate and empathetic. What a beautiful thing to have in life if what one speaks can be both affirmative as well as affectionate.

I hope that you get to experience this blessing too if you decide to not leave this as simply a read and use it to propel you into action too. As you allow yourself this gift of slowing down, I wish you stay safe and stay happy.

You must think through and decide what works best for you.

IV

An Interesting Life

Life! Such an uncomplicated thing in itself. Yet, many of us cannot help but turn it into a difficult puzzle that always has a piece or two missings. And the biggest irony of it is we do not even acknowledge that we are complicating it when asked why we do it. 'Not me!' is our almost automated response.

The episode that I am now going to narrate belongs to a week in my life when everything was quite eventful for me on the personal front. The week had had a rightful mix of happy and not-too-easy moments. I had met a lot of happy and a few sad faces. Some friends had come closer, and some could not share the warmth. All of this was what had made life so interesting. Amidst this entered a client, in my interaction with whom, the word 'interesting' stole the show.

Interesting! Yes, that is the word which we must always strive to look for in our lives. Instead, what I see with many of my clients and even some people that I know in my own life is that they associate words like good or bad, happy or sad, and easy or difficult, as soon as it comes to talking or thinking about life.

The reality is that life needs to be a mix of all of these words. A life that does not see all of these wonderful experiences can never be called a fulfilled life. And the last thing we can associate with such a living is to call it interesting.

Anyway, circling back to the client: It was a new client interaction, and as is normally the case, we had planned to have a generic know-each-other kind of talk before we even get to the details of what issues the person might be facing, and what must be done to sail through.

The conversation lasted for about twenty-five minutes, and that eventually also became the first and the last conversation we had about anything related to a client and a coaching relationship.

After five minutes of a generic introduction, the person went straight into sharing some experiences of his life which made him think about the endless troubles he had faced since the beginning of time. These experiences and the unease that they brought had somehow convinced him that he was not blessed with a good life. From what I could sense, his thoughts were hammering inside his mind in all directions — from feeling trapped in some sort of a *karma* cycle to thinking that he is a result of some sort of ill-fate, there were obviously many possible explanations he had about why he had gone through what he had gone through.

One peculiar thing that I could not help but notice was that he always supported any explanation he was giving with a real-life example. His intent, as I could gauge, was to make me confident that all that he was sharing was not a figment of his imagination, but his reality.

And the very fact that he quoted all those experiences made me understand that he actually was living such a blessed life. All that he was missing was the right perspective as to how to look at it all. The reason that was making his life seemingly unfortunate for him was exactly what made it fortunate for me to understand his issues better. Issues? No, I think I should just call it 'an issue'. And that issue was not being able to look at how interesting his life was.

The twenty-five minutes had him speaking for about twenty minutes and the remaining time was used by me to just make him leave the tight spot he had placed himself into, and shift to a place where he can look at all the same realities of his but with a different perspective.

It is only through this change of perspective that he was able to shift his focus and see how he had developed through all these experiences he had had in life. It all changed from being difficult, bad, sad, and tough, to being interesting. And once that shift happens for anyone, life becomes a blessing.

I am sure if we all take the various phases of our journey in our stride and endeavor to seek a life that is interesting rather than easy, we will see that our true evolution is rooted in a life which has its ups and downs.

It is lifeless that floats! The one which can be drowned can eventually swim through also.

A life that does not see all of these wonderful experiences can never be called a fulfilled life.

V

Expect the Right Thing the Right Way

If you expect disappointment, you can never really be disappointed.

This is a very famous dialogue from a Hollywood movie series. I myself have heard this being used, both casually as well as seriously, in many of the conversations around me. Thankfully, this dialogue has never been directed at me with seriousness ever, but only to create a humorously dramatic effect in a conversation.

But the very fact that I realize the impact such a medium can have on our mindsets makes me think about the relevance and rationality of this statement.

Disappointment to me, no matter how it comes, is not something which can be categorized as any close to life affirming. And what do I mean by life affirming? Life affirming is anything that uplifts us, anything that makes us hold life with the positive focus that it deserves, anything that helps us connect with our highest version of self. Disappointment, for sure, is not that.

And when I think further and deeper into the statement, I realize that there are actually two aspects to it that make me not find any synchronization with preparing oneself for disappointment.

The first and foremost is the one that goes in total alignment with how I like to live my life. I sincerely believe that our focus in life and expectation from it should always be only and only thoughts which are life affirming and life contributing.

I have learned through many experiences that our attitude towards life is what finally decides the kind of life we get to experience. And if our approach towards it is to be prepared for disappointments, then God save us, for we would have started living the disappointment much before something would have turned out to be that way for us.

Isn't it ironic? Just because we are not totally sure of the outcome, we prepare ourselves for the worst so that we do not feel the blow as adversely as it would have hit us if we were not prepared for it.

We keep our buffer system active to presume failure to come to us. A bigger irony is what if that failure never happens? What a waste of our mind space, our time, and our life would that be!

What do we gain then by allowing a *kafila* of negative energies to float around us when all that we were destined to get was only and only positive?

Think about it for a moment; and I am sure that you would only want to soak in breaths filled with positivity from here on!

Directing my attention now to the second aspect of the statement that I do not resonate with. A huge reason that makes me not align with this dialogue is my belief that the universe responds to the energy we emit out.

To explain it in simple terms, I strongly feel that we attract all that we prepare ourselves for. This belief finds its roots in multiple experiences that I have witnessed in my life and in the lives of those around me.

I place my firm faith in how the universe aligns to our best intentions, and our most honest and our most sincere desires for our life. And if that is the case, the last thing I want for myself and for those around me is to communicate to the universe through our words, our thoughts, or our actions that we are prepared for disappointment.

In fact — to be honest — leave being prepared for disappointments, I don't even want the universe to know that I know a word or a feeling like 'disappointment' exists.

I find myself short of words in explaining how strongly I think that life should be lived only on optimism and positive manifestation. Don't take me wrong — I am not saying that we should not handle the challenges that come our way realistically.

All I am asking is why should we consciously try to operate from a place of fear and hurt. Why can't we expect good and delicious things to happen to us? Why can't we trust that our positive focus will help us overcome any 'not-so-desired' thing that comes to us? Why do we have to prepare ourselves for tough times by already living the tough times? Why can't we use our good times to fill us with immense strength and resolve to be able to surf on even the toughest of waves with joy, love, and playfulness?

The universe responds to the energy we emit out.

VI

Positive Focus

In my experience of about a thousand plus hours of coaching and mentoring, if there is one belief that has resurfaced again and again, it is that what we focus on expands. My conviction that our thoughts create our reality has been reaffirmed numerous times, without failing even once. Such is the power of our own focus.

And when it is such a powerful thing, it makes complete sense that in whatever situation we may be in, we must not allow positive focus to not be our partner.

About a couple of months back, I encountered a situation in my own life when things didn't turn out how I expected them to be. What happened as a result of that was a challenge for me to ensure that things do not go wrong further. I did not have any immediate solution in sight. And the easiest choice I had was to take the route of sulking about the problem. It was then that my belief of holding on to positive focus helped me create magic.

I knew the importance of ensuring that things do not get worse, and thus rather than thinking about the seemingly obvious questions like why did it happen, what all will it lead to now, and how will it impact my being, what I directed myself towards was to ensure that the challenge was addressed in the most appropriate manner.

The most effective way of making that happen was to shift my focus to a different set of questions; questions that sounded like what good gets created getting into the solution, how wonderful life would be when this challenge does not exist anymore, what wonderfulness can I create by removing this obstacle.

And this shift in focus from the problem to the solution, from the negative to the positive is what energised each cell in my body to work towards ensuring that the situation is turned on its head in the best possible and fastest manner. This alignment between our being and our doing happens when we start to have a positive focus about things.

Though I have shared about one such situation that I encountered, the same has been my experience with countless situations that my clients have come across in their own lives. And with not even one experience that is otherwise — I, without any doubt, follow the dual mantra of having a positive focus and believing that what we focus on expands in life. This mantra has helped me transform my thoughts, my actions, my reactions and live a fulfilled and joyous life.

And while I have shared my experience with a lot of people, many have also benefited from the three-step approach that I have brought to their knowledge to increase the positivity quotient in their own lives. It is simple and gives sure results. The only thing it needs is constant and conscious practice.

The three steps to build positive focus are: The first step is to pause and acknowledge the complete truth about any situation in life. This is important because we generally react or act in a situation without developing a complete understanding of it. Two things that being mindful helps us significantly achieve are understanding what situation has been presented to us and how we must present ourselves to the situation. This short but mindful pause helps us offer our most desired version as per the situation.

The next step is to shift our focus to the positive side of the whole thing. This is what I call developing the habit of positive focus. Examples of positive focus can be what best I can create with the situation at hand, how a positive approach enables me to handle the situation better, and what reality I create for myself by ensuring that everything is taken care of well. All these thoughts activate the positivity in our minds and eventually help us shift our focus from the problem to the solution.

The last step then is to introspect and reflect upon the strengths and skills that we possess that can ensure our best version being presented to the situation. We all must be aware of our own strengths that enable us to create positive outcomes in all the situations and challenges we come across. Bringing these strengths to our active awareness is a habit that we all must develop.

I firmly believe that these three simple yet profound steps are a magical route to the positivity in life that many of us keep looking for.

My belief of holding on to positive focus helped me create magic.

VII
Happiness Explained

On a piece of paper were written two of my thoughts:

"If we seek only happy times, we are in some way wanting a life that is not lived to its fullest. Completeness of life is in seeing all its forms."

and

"You need to just make a decision to be happy. And rest, the universe will take care. Give life a new festive start."

A friend of mine read the thoughts and expressed that they were contradictory. According to her, while I was advocating not seeking only happiness in one of them, I was talking about deciding to always be happy in the other one.

The first thought talks about 'we not living to the fullest if we seek only happy times from our lives'. What I have referred to in that thought is the act of chasing happy moments. It is about that mad rush of only looking for things, places, people, moments, which will be able to give us happiness. What I have experienced in my own life is that relating happiness to something which is outside of us is the biggest irony. It is a trap to be looking for and associating happiness to anything and everything which works like a pleasantness creating machine and works to provide us with some lighter and relaxed moments.

Unfortunately, what it does is to not only make our happiness dependent on something or someone, but also most of the time eludes us from believing that we can be happy without them. It is in this very act of SEEKING that we give ourselves the message of NOT HAVING. This is the best representation of what is meant when it is said that the grass seems greener on the other side.

A life that comprises all different kinds of experiences and makes us capable of finding happiness in whatever situation we find ourselves in is truly a meaningful life.

This is where the first thought concludes and the second thought begins to expand.

We cannot always have situations that match or support our desires. Thus, what I have talked about in the second thought is to make a decision of being happy in the NOW, no matter what. This obviously would require us to stop making our happiness dependent on something happening in a certain way or someone behaving in a specific manner.

Happiness is something that should and must only be originating from within us. No matter what life throws at us or what we may have seen in the past, or even whatever we can assume will happen to us in our future, our happiness should be connected to only that which is within us. I have seen it for myself, and for many others whom I have coached, that the decision to be happy not only makes us live the challenges of our life better, but eventually even starts to present us with more such situations that justify the happy state we are in.

Thus, rather than basing our happiness onto something which may or may not happen, a decision to always hang on to happiness will bring to us from within us that which we were expecting to be brought to us from somewhere outside.

I am all for acknowledging the challenges that come our way — at times in the form of people and at other times with connection to things. However, what we must know is that what we seek from outside already lies within us. And being happy is what we all are naturally made to be. Trying to be anything else is making an extra effort to suppress that natural happy self of ours, which if allowed, will sprout on its own with no major effort.

I wish that each one of us can decide to work on finding that happiness within us. There is no denying that it might have hidden itself deep inside somewhere, because of all the damage that we might have tried to do until now. But the good news is that it will still be unharmed and will reveal itself in all its glory and magnificence when given a supportive and loving hand to unleash itself.

Finding happiness in whatever situation we find ourselves in is truly a meaningful life.

VIII

Life — What a Beauty!

Easier said than done: A response that I receive from several people when we are engaging in a dialogue about life. While I completely and wholeheartedly understand the unique sentiment behind this statement, an almost instinctive reply that I find myself giving people is that everything becomes effortless and easier with practice.

I do not think that practice makes us perfect — perfection seems like a utopian idea. But I do strongly believe that practice makes us better than before. It is this journey of becoming better that we must strive to continue treading on.

Perfection is just a perceived stage which loses its sheen as soon as we reach there. Have we not experienced those things that we believe will give us ultimate satisfaction, eventually turning into a milestone for another destination to be reached? Have we not ever been guilty of 'the grass is always greener on the other side' syndrome? Have we not felt that there is more and more to be achieved and that there is more and more to be done? Most likely, at some point in our lives, yes!

Do I live a life which is all sorted? Obviously not!

Do I face challenges in my life? Almost every day!

Do I feel that at times things get a bit difficult to handle? Quite often!

Then how do I say all those things which I speak in my dialogue about life? Does it not prove that it is easier to speak than to do? Well!

My belief and practice of it tell me that it is all about the way you look at life. A good life will keep throwing surprises at you all the time. At times they will be pleasant surprises, and at times they will take the shape and form of challenges. And that is what keeps life interesting. Isn't it? It is about what you decide to do with these gifts of life, which defines how it becomes for you.

In my case, though it has been quite a journey, I experience a stage where, more often than not, I choose to make things easy. It is a persistent endeavour to ensure that life is treated well, and all that it presents is received and acknowledged in its totality with utmost grace. And it is this very decision that makes me say that everything becomes effortless and easier with practice.

Making life easy, is by no means, taking life easy. This is an important distinction to make. And we must understand that it is actually in trying to take life easy that we make things difficult for us.

Life, for its grandeur, demands its rightful share of mindfulness and attention from all of us. And for those who do not heed to its demand, it does get difficult. The best thing in all of this is that the attention that life wants from us does not require us to focus anywhere outside.

Life, how we see it happening around us, is nothing but a reflection of what happens inside of us. Taking it easy is when we move away from ourselves, and making it easy is when we focus inwards and explore our own hidden gems to make this life a beautiful one.

I relate much to people who find it difficult to do this because that is the path that I have also walked in my life. And the very fact that I could walk past that and start making swift moves to manoeuvre through the course of life makes me confident that everyone else can do it too.

All we need is a resolve to ensure that we take charge of our life. And the only way we can take charge is by deciding how we respond internally to whatever happens outside of us.

To all those who still wonder if it is possible or not, I just want to say I used to have similar questions arising in my mind. And somewhere along the journey, those questions have been replaced by many beautiful answers.

Get up and create a life that you wish for yourself as I leave you with this thought that I have always found quite inspiring:

"Do not let anything — people, places, circumstances — pull you in their storm. Pull them into your peace instead."

It is this journey of becoming better that we must strive to continue treading on.

IX
Living in the Moment

Living in the moment has been the theme of my life for quite some time now. If I say, this is what has primarily driven my last few years, I think I would be giving the best description of how I have lived my life off late.

The time I am going to refer to in this narration is when I was traveling far, far away from home. During this time, there were many things happening that were 'first-timers', that carried with them no past reference, and the unfolding of which only the future could tell.

Uncertainty was knocking at the door more rigorously than ever. So, if living in the moment was not a practice that I would have been mindful of, I am sure the thoughts about the past and the future would have had an adverse impact on me.

They would have clawed on to me and pulled me into the loophole of mentally made-up scenarios. They would have made me imagine all things that could possibly go against me and may have put me in a zone of confusion, unpreparedness, and chaos.

Anyway, that was not meant to be. And all that I had done during this time was to live each moment to its fullest and embrace all that it brought for me. Everyday became a new learning and turned into an opportunity to see and experience something new.

Not that everything came as a pleasant surprise. There were times when the need was to manoeuver through the challenges presented by the unknown and the unfamiliar.

The key in such moments was to not get baffled by it and let the phase pass by. This awareness that it all is momentary helped me live it well while acknowledging it fully, yet not immersing myself into it beyond what is required.

My intention behind sharing about this particular time of my life is that I have heard from many of you that sometimes the practice of living in the moment is not something which comes very naturally.

And the time when living in the moment does not come naturally to us is when we precisely need to not rush for it. Just being mindful of it will eventually make it happen for us, as the benefits it carries are huge enough to pull anyone to start getting friendly with it.

Our past, as well as our future, are both very important parts of our lives, and at no moment which is considered as present, we can deny the importance of the time gone by or the times coming ahead.

However, what we must do is to not allow any of these to overshadow what we have in our hands currently. And this honoring of the now is what is called living in the moment.

This practice has helped me allow my past to stay where it belongs, and let my future show up to me when it is its time. And what has happened as a result is that both my past as well as my future get their deserved space in my life.

Peace and calmness are two of the blessings which show up by themselves as soon as we start to practice living in the moment. And it is these two that finally lead to joy showing up itself, making what we are living currently as our happy times.

What a simple recipe to have happiness in our life in the present, no matter whatever we may have seen in the past, or whatever we may be anticipating the future to be for us.

No wonder, the belief in its strength increases on its own when we first practice it consciously and see what it brings up before it becomes a part of our nature and happens subconsciously for us.

Life will keep on throwing its challenges, and some of them may even make it nearly impossible for us to be able to live in the moment. What we must ensure in such times is to tell ourselves that some small setbacks do not make us a total failure.

And whatever it takes to live a life that is fulfilled and contented in its present moment is a gift we all were born with. All that we need to do is to find that support system which helps us get up and get back, no matter how many times we fail in our endeavor of living in the moment.

This honoring of the now is what is called living in the moment.

X

The Delicate Balance

All the world's a stage; and all the men and women merely players!

While some gulped down these words as a part of their course textbook, others savoured them for the sheer love of literature – either way these iconic lines penned down by Shakespeare have been a part of many a life.

Why are we talking about the world and the stage, you may ask? The anecdote I am going to share here is from a time in my life when work was keeping me in a constant travel mode. It was during one of those trips that the United Arab Emirates happened to become my host for about 20 days. Somewhere amidst the official commitments, I managed to create time for treating myself with a visit to one of the major tourist attractions of Dubai, 'Global Village'.

This is a place that is frequented by many, both for shopping as well as experiencing the culture of various nationalities across the globe. In my endeavour to explore the traditions and heritage of around seven billion people who give meaning as well as depth to the longitudes and latitudes on the world map, I witnessed performances by some of the most spectacular artists from different countries.

Each performance that I encountered was enveloped by its own unique aura yet there were two of them that instantly started engaging and collaborating with my mind.

The first one of these two performances was a dance sequence presented by a group of men from Yemen. Their performance had all nuances of a magnificent one: great moves, soulful music, and soothing costumes. However, more than anything else, it was the PASSION and playful energy that was oozing out of the artists in the performance that invigorated me the most.

I am quite certain that there was a lead in the troupe of these Yemen men, as is the case in almost all dance groups. However, as an audience, it was nearly impossible to be able to put my finger on who that leader was, as the passion of one equally complemented and matched with the finesse of the others.

Their performance, which I am sure they practiced and put together every single day as a routine, was an extraordinary example of the freshness that passion can give birth to even in the most repetitive aspects of our lives.

Another important lesson I picked up from the Yemen men was that our best comes out when the people who surround us are involved and driven with the same degree of passion, intensity, and love as us in the space we share with them. This alliance could be personal or professional; we may call it teamwork or a healthy relationship, it matters not. The truth is that it is only through associations driven by shared passion that we can unleash the power which comes from collectively focusing on what excites us.

Coming to the second act that stirred my thoughts that day! It was a performance given by two very young boys in the Chinese pavilion. My initial impression of these boys was quite far from being amazed by them. This was because as these boys entered the stage, they looked overtly stern, intense, and restrained. Instead of greeting or smiling at the audience, these boys appeared to be preoccupied and contained in their own inner world making me assume that it was going to be a dull performance by two people who didn't really enjoy their work.

However, within the first 30 seconds of their performance itself, my perspective of them drastically changed. The boys had chosen to put together a performance with a series of complex balancing acts that made jaws drop. It, undoubtedly, required dexterous skills, immense amounts of concentration, and out-of-the-world synchronisation. They naturally didn't have any room for wasting their focus on gestures such as smiling at the audience or greeting them.

Their performance came as an important reminder that while it is important to be guided by passion, there are times when sustaining the goals driven by this passion requires us to prepare ourselves mentally and physically for the challenges. Being focussed without any distractions can be a great help in such times.

So, let us strive to establish in our day to day lives the delicate balance between our passion and our focus – to give in all that we can to offer wings to our dreams but to hold back all that we must to sustain them!

It is only through associations driven by shared passion that we can unleash the power which comes from collectively focusing on what excites us.

The ‘We’ in ‘Me’

XI

Beyond Perfection

A million books on the topic; a million ideas to stir the mind and just as many people in the pursuit to unravel, layer by layer, the various nuances of their relationships – yet none having a sure and universal response to what is it that really works.

To each his own! This is why a message that I received from a very close friend urging me to share my opinion on something concerning relationships set me to serious thinking. His question: Does it affect a relationship if one of the partners has a higher level of intellect than the other?

Since one shoe does not fit all, I tried to view and understand the point of contention from a much more nurturing, expanding, and observing lens to ensure my reply to him takes into account all relevant perspectives.

The almost instant answer that found its way to me was a definitive 'No' – a difference of intellect would not seem important enough to have an effect on a relationship because from where I see it the emotions corresponding to love operate from a space much further away from the zones of our mental faculty.

By this I mean that most people do not burden the left side of their brain when it comes to their loved ones. Love is a creative process; thus, it is only natural for us to be experimenting with the more imaginative, more unreal side of our brains – the right brain.

Paying attention to this very tendency of not putting to use the rational, analytical, and logical side of our brains when it comes to relationships revealed for me the other side of the story, or should I say the other side of my reply to my friend.

And what is this other side of the story? Not relying on the left sides of our brain where it concerns our loved ones somehow also implies intentionally or unintentionally overlooking the way the difference that ACTUALLY EXISTS in thoughts, intellect, or attitudes is shaping our relationship.

To find a balanced ground, I feel that – instead of overlooking or avoiding it – it is much wiser to acknowledge the difference that exists in the platter of thoughts or assortment of intellects between partners. The endeavour must be to cultivate a space where two people can be upfront about these differences and can openly discuss the same.

Having a discourse of such nature is bound to find its route through some uneasy conversations, bumpy reality checks, and not so 'aesthetically appealing' views; but eventually what the partners would surely find germinating at every step through this meaningful process are the seeds of honesty; a value that must form the very breath and essence of such relationships.

As a partner, it should be our eternal desire to ensure that our connected soul understands the limitations that any one of us possesses and either acknowledges what this gap creates or works to bridge that distance by laying the foundation of understanding.

Relationships, particularly a very special few, deserve our cent percent loyalty and supreme truthfulness. Making our partner comprehend and admit their limitations as much as their capabilities is an important element of making them respect them for who they are; by showing them that it is possible to love them even with their boundaries.

Yes, differences of intellect do exist between partners, but how and whether at all it impacts and affects our relationship is solely dependent on the way we choose to respond to it.

This is what determines if our EQ can actually keep up with our IQ; or are these just utopian ideas that we have passed by as distant ideals without incorporating them as a part of our core.

So, let us strive to understand, acknowledge, and celebrate the differences between us and our partners, and as a result experience how two parts that are differently incomplete make a complete whole that is beyond perfection!

The endeavour must be to cultivate a space where two people can be upfront about these differences and can openly discuss the same.

XII

The Curious Case of Worthiness

When you skim through different texts to find what eminent poets and authors have to say about travel, chances are you would stumble on romanticised ideas about the adventures and beauty associated with it. Rarely will you find a poet writing with the same passion about the long yet realistic security checks and countless scanners awaiting one at the airport. Hardly will you find a writer writing with the same romanticism about the ordeals of staying seated at a place in the aircraft for hours altogether.

Regardless of what your personal feelings may be about airport routines, there are times when there is no escape from this travel mode. On occasions such as these, I usually like to find adventure in monotony by observing people around me.

It was during one of these habitual recces of my surroundings on a flight that my attention was captured by an elderly couple who was travelling on the same aircraft as mine. Let us just say that the man had so much enigma stored within his aura that his body was overwhelmed by it, and hence, he used a wheelchair at all times and was highly restricted in his body movements. The lady, on the other hand, carried herself with such dignity that she – without a word, without an action – almost instantly earned respect.

I could not help but notice the ease with which the woman was escorting her partner and was helping him being manoeuvred in his designated seat. Almost 30 minutes into the flight when the crew started serving food and beverages, I observed the woman carefully and patiently arranging the man's meal on the table in front of him, without any hint of restlessness, agitation, or impatience to free up the airhostess. When the arrangements were made to her satisfaction, she thanked the air hostess with the man briefly nodding his head in synchronicity. The woman then began to feed the man as one would feed a little child. She was simultaneously talking about something that was evidently making the man laugh. She was chuckling herself throughout.

Finally, as they were ready to discard the waste and clean the left-overs, the movements of the woman and the man were so harmonized that I felt as if I was watching a dance sequence.

Almost an hour into the flight when everyone was ready to settle – the sleepers were ready to sleep, the readers were ready to read, the workaholics were ready to work, and the movie watchers were ready to watch movies, I was curious to see how the couple would plan to spend their time. And there it was – a sight to behold!

The lady was impeccably resting her head on the shoulders of her man; her face radiating and making obvious the serenity and the security she was feeling within. The man, despite his physical condition, was somehow magically able to make room for his woman.

And there I was left sleepless and smiling by the simplicity of the whole incident wondering how ridiculously we scrutinise our relationships and day-to-day lives under the tainted lens of power dynamics – trying to establish more authority, position, and worth over the other when instead we do have the effortless choice of respecting the space of the other and taking pride in the space that we own and then creating a beautiful, harmonized space together.

In this case, some would see the man being dependent on the woman; others would call the woman being bound by responsibilities of matrimony; and then there would be some like me who would be able to see two individuals thriving through the circumstances thrown at them and empowering each other by taking charge when needed and giving in when required.

How different this narrative would have been if the lady would have been feeling burdened by responsibilities! How different the narrative would have been if the man would have been viewing himself less in control!

How uncomplicated life becomes when we understand and accept each one's role in our lives and our role in the lives of people around us! How empowering and peaceful life becomes when all that we do with ourselves and the other is guided by love!

Whichever situation we may be in, both responsibility and authority would always come attached to it. How we interpret and work around this responsibility as well as authority depends on our free will which in turn determines the quality of our thoughts and life.

Peace, happiness, and contentment come to those who honour their own space and also that of others. 'Respecting the authority of others as we understand our responsibility' and 'Respecting the responsibility of others as we understand our authority' is a sign of an individual who is both gracious and grateful.

Empowering each other by taking charge when needed and giving in when required.

XIII
The Faith of Happiness

Happiness, I believe, is a shield against anything harsh and cruel in this world. I consider the smiles which reach our eyes and the laughter which reaches our heart as the most prosperous of blessings anyone can ever be endowed with. Thus, it should not come as a revelation if I tell you that I take personal interest in ensuring that I as well as those who matter to me are living the festive times to their fullest.

The more I am growing and understanding life as an individual, the more I am coming to realise how significant and important these symbols of celebrations are in our lives. Irrespective of the challenges and circumstances that life may be hurling at us, these celebrations knock at our doors as reminders of hope, joy, light, and love.

One particular Christmas, as I opened the abode of my heart to exchange Christmas greetings with my near and dear ones, I felt extremely fortunate and grateful by the way my love was reciprocated with sincere wishes and blessings adding to the richness of my life. With all the joy that came to greet me on Christmas accompanied my forever friend 'reflection'.

Where and how did I find the scope to introspect in the middle of the pepped up times, you may ask? Well, the credit goes to some unusual responses that I received on my tailor-made festive messages. A few on my list responded back to my 'Merry Christmas' with their 'Jai Shree Ram'. Before you give any religious connotations to the entire episode and start to think whether 'Jai Shree Ram' was the right thing to say or not, let me tell you that I have no biased preferences or favourites between Christ and Ram. I am equally and insanely in love with both.

My reflection came more in terms of why an obvious wish was not sent back to me. Though I did reciprocate the wish respecting the sentiments of the sender, I could not help but wonder what was the apprehension that the sender had in admitting that it was Christ's birthday that day and not Ram Ji's?

I deliberated: Is this response of the sender due to the affinity towards their own religion? Or wait! Is it originating out of an intent to not even acknowledge the religion and faith of others? Is it a symbol of self-pride? Or is it a consequence of a bloated ego that is too fearful and fragile? I am sure those who are inclined to respond this way may have their reasons to back up their actions.

But something in me asks me, is it really worth it - to be overshadowed so much by your own beliefs that you shut your doors to the joy that anything out of your beliefs could bring you? I mean what is the point in finding bitterness in happiness. Why are we so unsure and insecure about our own faith that we get threatened at the slightest mention of any other faith?

Why can't we be simply mindful and grateful for what we are and what all we have so that we are able to eventually find our smiles in those of others and create celebrations all around?

I just hope that such people, like a lot many of us who acknowledge the blessings of diversity and uniqueness, get to see happiness that stands beside them waiting for its hand to be held and walked along. I hope that everyone becomes capable enough of finding their corner of happiness in the house full of smiles that they are blessed with.

I am reminded of what a dear friend of mine (who hails from a different religion) once told me while taking Prasad from a temple, "For me, the only thing that matters is to satisfy my craving for sweets. Whether the sweet comes from a shop or a place of religion, I eat it with the same happiness and gratitude as I would always do."

Every festive season and each day of our lives, I hope we find our faith in happiness - making our faith of happiness.

These celebrations knock at our doors as reminders of hope, joy, light, and love.

XIV
You are the Love

Love is a give and take! For how long can one keep giving love if it is not reciprocated? This is a statement and a question that I often get presented with.

Though I am extremely clear about my own thoughts about the matter, the very fact that the statement and the question arise make me reflect deeper, and see what generally gets triggered in the majority of people when the discussion is around the emotion of love.

The one big revelation which I arrived at is that the very premise on which love should be based on is hugely misunderstood. Love, which is and should be the purest form of selflessness, is vastly construed as something that we either give to someone or take from someone. An emotion that was supposed to have nothing connected to outside of us has become so externally focused that the very essence of it has been lost.

Love is turned into a practice, which has — as a consequence — become an act of performing and behaving in a certain manner, which makes us believe that it is something getting transferred or transmitted from one to another. And just because it is being given out, there comes an expectation of it being received also. Making others feel loved has become an area of responsibility, added to so many other responsibilities of worldly matters out there. Feeling loved is no more based on something which is all inside of us, but has become dependent on what we receive from something or someone outside of us.

Love is what we are all about. Love is what originates and grows within us. Attraction, liking, and appreciation for something or someone can be dependent on things that are external to us, but I don't know of even one person who could be made to love someone unless it did not originate from within their own self. And just because we, as humans, are most distant from our own selves, we find it easy to assign an external motivation to the love that we feel towards what is outside of us. This very reason of having assigned the cause of love being originated because of something outside of us becomes responsible for love to either grow or diminish because of external factors.

We believe that the love we feel for someone is being given by us to them, and thus in return we also feel that it is either being given back or not being reciprocated. My various experiences of my own life and of those that I have been blessed to be a part of has made me understand that what we call love within us never leaves us, or goes to someone else. It is a feeling that originates within us, grows within us, and then thrives within us only, making us a person who is affectionate and caring towards others. Likewise, there is no love from anywhere outside of us that enters within us, and makes us feel good about ourselves and feel loved. What we know of as love existing between two individuals for each other is simply love that exists within two individuals.

We are neither the givers nor the takers of what love is. We are where that love is born, and we are where that love flourishes. And in some cases, if it does not serve what we are, we see that the same love ceases to exist. All that we do is assign a reason to it which is outside of us in order to not bend our perception of what love is all about.

Feeling in love with someone is completely an independent feeling of ours. Likewise, others also have their own respective feelings. It, indeed, is a beautiful thing if these two independent feelings complement each other. What it creates is an environment within us where our own love grows and is nourished making us more loving and caring. But while it must be cherished, it should not be dependent on anything external.

If there is any give and take in love, it is about GIVING ourselves the acknowledgement that we carry love within ourselves and TAKING pride through ourselves that we allow it to grow and flourish within us.

I sincerely hope that we all acknowledge what love truly is and understand all its magnificence that gets created within us when we understand that it is independent of anything or anyone that is outside of us.

Soak into this lovely feeling of being love!

We find it easy to assign an external motivation to the love that we feel towards what is outside of us.

XV

Own the True You

When life throws things at you, you can either duck to let it pass or catch them to have a rendezvous and see what made all that come to you. In my case, I almost always decide on the latter.

I am well aware that I am getting into a bare-all mode here, but that is what I feel defines who I am truly. To put myself into a zone of vulnerability is what makes me feel I am living the right way. And so, not being afraid of judgements, not being sceptical of reactions, I am here sharing one of the most profound experiences of my life..

It all started when someone very-very close to me found out that I was not sharing the complete truth about what I was doing. And how upon being sure that I was not, he confronted me with what all he already knew about the various situations. Needless to say, things didn't turn up well, and it led to a good amount of unpleasantness. And that too at a level, where we walked out on each other, vowing never to meet again.

Anyway, my focus is not to talk about how the other person reacted, and what was right or wrong in his actions. Instead, what I am trying to achieve here is to call out loud what was my contribution to all that got messed up. My actual instant and the impulsive reaction was to bring to my mind all the things that were done by the other person, that led to me being untruthful and not sharing things as they were. I gave myself all the reasons and reminded myself of all the possible instances in the past when he was unable to accept and honour the truth about a situation when it was shared by me most honestly. That mode of thinking stayed in me for about a day, when I kept on looking at the things that were outside of me. Not that I was ever wanting to justify what I did, but what I realized was that my focus was still not completely on why and what led me to become and behave in a manner which was nowhere close to what I truly am or what I honestly aspire to be.

Maybe it was divine interference that happened the next day to make me realize what I was focusing on, and also tell me that it was nowhere in alignment with the purpose for which I live my life or the values that I believe drive who I am. AND BANG! There, in a flash of a second, as if my world turned upside down, and all my focus and thoughts got concentrated on what was my contribution and who was I being in all this.

What that did was to evaporate any thought of finding any excuse, creating any reasons, looking for anyone's actions that led me to not being truthful to someone. And all that remained was, what could I have done to be strong enough to behold honesty? What made me go weak in not telling the truth when I had no intention of cheating on that other person? What did I create in my reality for thinking that my truth cannot be understood? What made me believe that I cannot put an effort into the truth to be accepted by everyone when there was nothing wrong involved in it? And what started with all these questions ended with just one answer: The ownership of what I was involved in lies completely on me.

This one acknowledgement was enough for my core to accept that whatever comes now as a result of my action, I must accept in its totality, and in no way, I want to ever justify what I did. Detaching myself from whatever thoughts made me act in a way that was not me, I know that nothing ever can make me go the wrong way again if I remain mindful of keeping the ownership of my actions and my talks in its completeness.

This feeling of taking charge of one's actions and decisions, though, brings a lot of responsibility on oneself, but is also immensely liberating. It did not only free me of finding reasons that were outside of me, it also made me independent to choose what I want to be from hereon.

For me, the choice was quite obvious, and that is to focus on how I never want to get into such a scenario again and to maintain that same love and gratitude towards that person who was at the receiving end of what was my weakness. As I take this opportunity to raise an apology to him through the universe, I am hoping that everyone who reads this, finds some time to experience what takes place inside of you when you take complete ownership of all the good and bad, right and wrong, that you ever were involved in.

On this note, I wish you cherish your empowered selves, and make sure that you find time to connect with your loved ones.

Whatever comes now as a result of my action, I must accept in its totality, and in no way, I want to ever justify what I did.

XVI
Measured Trust

Trust – an exceedingly delicate word and an equally fragile emotion. Somewhere in the blueprints of time, we have all at least once gone through the pain of being a victim of breach of trust. Chances also are that the ebb and flow of life has at least once put us on the other end where we have been accused of not living up to someone's trust.

I myself have experienced and endured both these sides; not just once but over and over. And, today when I reflect and rendezvous with the delicate notions of trust, I am able to safely conclude that most episodes involving breach of trust aren't really about any breach. They are, in fact, only about the miscalculated difference between two people's ideas and understanding of what they term as 'trust'.

In my opinion, just like any other miscalculation, the discrepancies revolving trust can always be reworked to a point of accuracy with some effort and some change in our approach. What I mean is that rather than trying to fit square pegs in round holes, we can avoid unnecessary discomfort by simply being realistic about answers to some very basic and crude questions such as: Can this person be trusted? If yes, what are the things I can trust this person for? To what degree can this person be trusted on the things I trust them with?

How does this help, you might ask? I firmly believe that once we make seeking answers to these questions a habit right at the beginning of our associations, being betrayed becomes out of question as our expectations as well as actions begin to be guided by a precise acceptance of what the other person is and is not capable of.

However, there is not even a slight doubt that getting to the answers for these questions requires a great deal of wisdom, dexterity, patience, intent, and determination. But, then, the effort is worth it; particularly when it can help us avoid the unpleasantness we may be led to if we choose to not be aware of who to trust, when to trust, and how much to trust.

So, how do we really implement this in our lives? The first step to take is to search our repertoire of experiences to decide whether or not we can trust a certain someone. While doing so, we must ensure that we are sincere and honest in our search for answers and are not overlooking or forgetting the flawed aspects of our relationship with someone; thus, making ourselves vulnerable to being victimized again. We must remember that while it is great to move forward and above the actual happenings that may have hurt us with respect to a person in the past, our motto must be to never let go of what the pain taught us so that we can transform it into a lesson for making our lives better in the present and the future.

After deciding on whether to trust a certain someone or not, the second step should be to find clarity about the things, situations, and aspects in which the other person can be trusted. It helps to be mindful that different people have different personalities; their actions are always driven by this inherent core. Being with someone for a longer period can help us understand how they are, and what is it that can and cannot be expected out of them. Once this is clear, to make life easier, it is always good to avoid getting into things with them which are on the NO TRUST list.

Last, but maybe the most important of all, is to define the extent of trust we can place on a certain someone. Though such an approach to life may seem way too demanding and methodological, but once practiced, it adds to the quality of both our lives as well as our relationships. Now, we can determine the extent to which we want to trust someone based on multiple aspects such as our equation with them, our willingness to expect more out of them even at the cost of disappointments, and of course the situations around.

Having done all of this, our endeavour must be to repeat the whole process again and again over consistent intervals, as people and situations both are dynamic, and change is what brings life to life.

I strongly believe that a process such as this must be an intrinsic element of all our relationships because hurt that could have been avoided and trust that got breached generally comes with collateral damage. By this, I mean that when we unconsciously but actively continue to be a part of mindless cracks in trust, we carry the baggage to affect even those people who should be cared for and trusted.

Thus, raise your awareness and enjoy your relationships by keeping the MEASURED TRUST alive!

Never let go of what the pain taught us so that we can transform it into a lesson

XVII

Cherish Your Blessings

The usual morning rituals. A cup of *chai.* A walk around the same old path. A habitual catch-up on the news. Work. Family time. Me time. Friends. On the face of it, my days were just routine.

Yet, this was a time in my life when only I knew that both ecstasy and challenges were playing a tug of war in my experiences to find their place within me. Moments of extreme high and moments of extreme trials were fighting for my attention, both trying to take an edge off the other.

It was a time of choices! I had to choose what to immerse myself into — Should my immersion be in the challenges? Or should it be in the strength that they awaken when the tests arrive.

Yes, the challenges did make me feel the weight for a while, but then it was the other side, which is that of ecstasy, strength, calmness and gratitude that I chose to place myself onto. While this is one of the episodes I have recollected and narrated here from my life, it is certainly not the only one.

I have always been a firm believer of and a strong advocate for a life which has both its ups and downs, both its happy and challenging moments. This faith in me comes from a thought of mine that with almost every challenge we face, we master the art of creating less and less space for complaints and more and more space for acknowledging the way the tests add up to our grander purpose.

I guess that it is this belief about the completeness of life which makes me come across such experiences every now and then. So yes, though every challenge will need to be taken care of, in the larger scheme of things, I take it all as a blessing.

Every time something like this happens and the way I respond to it, I look around to see what gives me the strength to sail through. And the only answer I get is the blessing I have in the form of people I have in my life. I am not someone who has an endless list of friends and acquaintances, and I am definitely not someone who socializes a lot or focuses on creating a network. But there can be no denying the fact that people who I am close to are indeed no less than blessings in my life.

Through my work, I meet different kinds of people who come to me for help in various aspects of their life. One thing which I always find common across all is that both their problems and their solutions lie either within them or are somehow connected to the people that they connect with. It is this very experience which strengthens my belief about the importance of honouring one's blessings, which come in the form of those who we connect with.

Yes, we do have our differences at times with our close ones too, and it is quite natural to not be able to relate to everything in them. The choice, then, is between focusing on that which disconnects and concentrating on that which we find a connection with. In life, it is so effortless to find faults and move away from people, but the real progress is when we acknowledge the uniqueness of all those around us and understand the importance of them being a part of us.

Though relationships and our connection with people is and will always remain a work in progress, what we must not overlook is the value that a presence brings to us.

We must remember that as we evolve in our life, everyone else around us also has their life experiences happening, and thus bringing about specific changes in them. Expecting someone to not have changed for good or expecting someone to stay the same just because we thought that was their best version are both wrong, and this is where we generally let go of these blessings that play a silent yet important part in our lives.

I genuinely believe a life that has a mix of good times and not so good times is the best experience possible. And it all becomes much better if we have people who can celebrate our good times and stand by us in our times of challenges.

It is a good habit to look around, pause, and acknowledge the presence of these gems in our life. Let us inculcate the habit in our life to feel grateful about these blessings, and also at times to let them know that they are cherished.

Remember, every word of encouragement and gratitude helps someone be a better version of themselves, and thus makes a positive impact on many more lives.

A life which has both its ups and downs, both its happy and challenging moments.

XVIII

The Love He Was, He Is . . .

Unconditional and unquestioned love! What does that even mean? Is true, undiluted love even possible? Whenever I find myself thinking these thoughts, almost naturally Veer comes up in my mind.

Veer was my four-legged brother who passed away a few years back. As every person who has ever owned a dog feels, Veer was no ordinary one. In fact, when I talk of him in past tense, it only pertains to his physical form. His essence, on the other hand, always stays with me. He stays.

It was Veer who showed me what the definition of love is. That which we seek and do much for to either receive or give can be so easily practiced is what I always saw in him. And I am consciously not saying that I learnt that from him because I know I have a long way to go before I could even see myself close enough to the kind of love he displayed.

This love was not only for me or my mother. I never saw even one person whom he met that did not get the same, intense, raw love from him, and even gave the same in return to him. Such was Veer's aura that anyone who ever got to meet him became his and made him theirs, including people who he met often and people who he met just once. There was never a 'getting to know' kind of phase for him. He instantly chose and created love around him, wherever and with whoever it was.

And this is one big learning for life which I have been trying to imbibe in my life as my way of saying 'Thank You' to Veer. I am still not there, but I promise him each time I try and fail to do so, that I will keep at it, and make him proud someday.

When I look back at his life, all I see is love and compassion. He had been a protector. He had been a source of strength. He had been a symbol of good times. And what he was and he remains is a representation of loving without boundaries.

He lived short, but he lived big. And though I know that I can never match his bigness, I wish that I am able to keep him close to me ever and always by being somewhat like what he was.

It is not that I get tears whenever I think of him. In fact, often, his thoughts bring a smile to me, and what that tells me is the lasting effects of the happiness he spread while he breathed. I must admit though, that I am writing this with tears in my eyes, as not missing him does not come easy.

My intention behind sharing about Veer was not only to pay a tribute to his life which carries on in his memories within each and every person who ever touched him. Or I should say, he ever touched. What I also intend is to pass on this thought of reflecting on the kind of love we practice in our lives.

It would be good and worth enough to ask ourselves if we have allowed any dilution of the quality of love in our lives. Are we even mindful of what love is? Are we actually calling something else with the name of love?

And though these questions may bring up replies which we feel either good or not so good about, the purpose behind asking them is to not feel bad if we see the quality of our love having got diluted. My sole intention and purpose, which stems from my belief that 'it is never late', is to see what comes up, and then allow what wants to happen.

It is not wrong if the love has changed to care. It is not wrong if love has given way to support. What is even wrong in a desire of someone having taken the place of what started with nothing but undiluted love? To me there is absolutely nothing wrong in any of these, as all of it also is our own reality. But yes, if these revelations create a desire to bring things back to how they were, to get back to the times when we practiced and experienced pure, undiluted love, then all I suggest is to grab this thought and hang on to it — Until it becomes a part of us again. I have no doubts that life will become magical yet again.

My thoughts and talks about Veer will never end. And so will the love that he left behind for me to experience and share it with the world out there. All I want to do right now is to send out all the love and affection to each one of you, and hope that you sense the warmth of its purity, which carries a hug from Veer too.

And what he was and he remains is a representation of loving without boundaries.

XIX
The Third Angle

Perspectives! Our personal, unique, and special way of understanding and making meaning out of the things, people, and situations around us. And if we look at it from a micro view, we will see that this is one of the biggest factors that defines the kind of life we decide to live.

I am consciously choosing my words here because I believe strongly that it is we who decide what perspective we want to have for something.

This decision can surely be either a conscious one or something which is driven unconsciously by the experiences we have been through. In most cases, it is the latter that influences how we perceive things.

And though experience is a great thing to have, sometimes we turn this very blessing into a nightmare. Sometimes what we allow it to do to us is something we need to be careful about.

It is important to acknowledge that not everything that we see with our eyes is true. And that is simply because our truth about it is nothing but just how we perceive it to be.

This is significant because it means that everything that we may have seen till now in our lives may or may not be true. This is because we carry within us not only the imprints of our own perceptions but also of many others too, as we get influenced by the experiences and opinions of others during our journey to where we are.

Why do I feel it is relevant to talk about perspectives? It is because of my own experiences with it in my life. Almost everything that happens in our relationships with ourselves as well as those with others has everything to do with just one word: perspective.

There have been many times in my life when things have been a roller-coaster in relationships. In moments such as these, I make it a point to consciously give myself some moments of reflection, detaching myself from the experience itself.

This helps me not to be biased and look at things only from my perspective. This also helps me watch out against the tendency of negating my perspective completely and looking at or accommodating things only from the other person's perspective because of my genuine love and care for them.

What happens in this kind of a reflection is that one gets to see the situation for what it is, and thus make sense of what wants to show up through this. Such a reflection helps us create an undiluted, pure, and safe space where we do not give any more or any less value to our unique way of looking at and understanding things, people, and situations.

I must admit that it is a very arduous path to walk on, and I am satisfied that I am able to stay on it for some bits and moments. However, I must also admit that the magic of this space is so deep and impactful that even a short stay here gives one so much clarity that seems to have been impossible to achieve if there was a bias attached to it.

The process involves a lot of courage and determination. Naturally so! After all, placing oneself away from a biased space can present many chances of either feeling ashamed or getting into the blame game.

But then if one has confidence in the purity of what you share with the situation, thing, or the person involved, it gives all the strength that is desired and required for this practice to happen. It helps you sail through the rough waters and eventually anchor yourself in a place that is truthful, authentic, and respectful of the third angle.

I must admit that I am still a work in progress with respect to this practice as I write about it today and share it with you. Yet, I have a very strong belief that I will be able to emerge as a much more righteous, truthful, understanding, and supportive being through it.

I hope and pray that we all get the strength to live life from a space that holds a huge possibility of allowing our blissful lives, in harmony with ourselves as well as others.

And as the saying goes, a shift in perspective opens a completely new set of unlimited possibilities.

We get influenced by the experiences and opinions of others during our journey to where we are.

XX
Perspective

Our own unique way of looking at things, that is what we know of what a perspective is. When I call it unique, it does mean that it cannot be influenced by the opinion of others. But the most important factors that create our perspectives are the experiences that we have had in our life, and the expectations we have.

It is our perspective about things, situations, and people that makes us experience things in the way that best suits our mindset, or expectations.

According to me, it is one of the greatest manipulators of our mind, that holds a space within us with our consent and then drives how we see our life as.

To elaborate on what I shared above, I would like to add reference to a movie I recently watched. The movie is about a cricket player who is shown to be fighting odds to regain and reestablish his career in cricket.

One of the scenes that made an impact on me was when the hero of the film completes his knock and comes back to the pavilion after a successful outing.

He saves the day for his team and everyone, except one of the head selectors, congratulates him on his success. The accolades are not only for his own personal knock, but also the fact that it saved his team from a loss and turned the result upside down.

To give a little background, the time he went to bat, his team was not in good shape and the need of the hour was to not lose further wickets and save the day by surviving. And that was the message given by everyone to this player, while he left for the pitch. 'Do not lose your wicket.'

The next 10 minutes of the movie was all about his flamboyant shots and huge sixes and great boundaries, and thus making it a great display of exciting batting. It did not only save the day for his team, but also turned the match in their favor.

While everyone congratulated this hero batsman and said, 'well played', the head selector asked him, 'Do you think you played well?' Your adventure had put the whole team at risk. What did I tell you?', to which the hero batsman replied, 'Sir, you told me to not lose the wicket. And I didn't.' And there it was. The next thing that came out of the selector's mouth was, 'Well played.'

Just a movie scene. But it tells us so much about perspective and how we look at life, and thus create our experiences. The intention of both the player and the selector was the same: 'Not to lose the wicket.' But their perception about what will make that happen differed, and thus created a different experience for both. The selector's perception about not losing the wicket was to play defensive, while the hero batsman's natural game was to attack and therefore, his perspective was to play his natural game if he must not lose his wicket.

Nothing wrong with either. But what it created was a very different experience for two individuals while the match was being played. While one was enjoying his batting, playing attacking shots to retain his wicket, the other person was always tense thinking that this was not the right way to preserve the wicket.

This was just a match, and that too in a movie. But in life as well, the exact same happens for us. Or I should say, the exact thing is created by us for ourselves. It is a very different thing when the desires are different, but when the similarity of what is desired also creates a different experience, mindfulness can totally help us avoid the unpleasantness.

A good way to do it is to step out of the self-zone at times, and look at things, situations, and people from an independent third perspective. This practice enables us to give a chance to look at our own perception of things from an outsider's view, and thus give it a chance to be molded for our best experience.

It is true that even the third perspective, which is outside of us, will have an impression of our self and won't be completely independent, but it still serves because it starts with an acknowledgement that our perspective is not the only perspective, and eventually it strengthens into a habit which is supported by our newer experiences which are much more joyous and fuller.

It tells us so much about perspective and how we look at life, and thus create our experiences.

Face to Face with Emotions

XXI
Enough and More

Once, a client of mine asked me a few questions. These were questions that had kept me thinking for a long time in my life. The questions were posed to me during a coaching session where emotions were running high and my client was able to make himself completely vulnerable.

Almost choking with feelings, he asked: For someone like me who has always been able to achieve whatever I have planned for myself, why is it that I am not able to feel satisfied ever in life? Why do I always want more and more? How do I break this cycle of setting new expectations and desires?

His honest predicament opened floodgates of flashbacks for me. The concern felt familiar. It was not the first time that I was hearing something like this from someone I was coaching.

Naturally, I did the best I could in my capacity as a coach to help him arrive at the answers that work for him by reflecting deep and accessing his own core. What amazed me was that the thoughts he came up with were pretty much in sync with what I also feel and think about the matter. That not only strengthened my own belief about the issue but also reaffirmed for me that humans carry so many commonalities even in our uniqueness.

Coming back to the question of not being satisfied, and always wanting more and more out of life. My thoughts about this are very clear, and it is that both things are independent of each other, and the problem only occurs when we start to associate them together.

Being satisfied or dissatisfied is more about how we feel about something that we have or have not achieved. Satisfaction is mostly the sense of fulfilment we experience when we feel complete about having gotten or done something.

It is only upon completion of a task or phase in life that we can gauge if what just passed by gave us a sense of satisfaction or not. If we feel good about it, it makes us satisfied, and if otherwise, we declare that we have been dissatisfied. Satisfaction, or the opposite of it, is always related to one thing: how we feel about that which occurred or happened.

On the other hand, wanting more out of your life is completely independent of if one is satisfied or not with what is around. I have known many people, who despite having achieved so much and being so satisfied with what they already have, still aspire for more out of their lives.

And I have also known a huge number of people, who despite not having enough and not being satisfied with what all they have been able to create, do not feel the urge of seeking more from their lives. Some always strive for more, and then there are those who always think of having enough.

All these experiences have made me believe one thing very strongly, and it is that wanting more and more out of your life is not a bad thing, given you are willing to give it all that it takes.

But it is equally important for us to feel satisfied and complete with whatever life has offered us till present. It is only when we feel grateful for what we have till now, we make ourselves and our lives prepared for receiving and creating more than we may want for ourselves.

My client came to me with a life situation that, according to him, was creating confusion in his head and was binding him down.

And though nothing changed externally in his situation, I was so happy that an internal shift had happened and what he carried back from the session with him was the feeling of being satisfied with his current reality coupled with his zeal to achieve more and more in his life.

I feel blessed that through my work, I can see people making huge strides forward in knowing themselves and meeting their core self. I hope that you also take some time out today and present yourself with reflection time to find satisfaction in what all you have, and know what and how much you want from your life ahead.

Humans carry so many commonalities even in our uniqueness.

XXII

The Happiness Quotient

All or nothing - a way of life most of us have begun to take pride in embracing. Finding a middle ground has started to appear almost as trespassing. For everything in our life, we enjoy it only when it fully fills our box and definition of completeness; and if not, we snub away whatever little we may be receiving of it. After all, we either want to experience all of it or none of it; there is no 'in-between'.

Seems like a solid resolve, doesn't it? Strong, without a doubt; but this very mindset becomes quite unyielding when we apply its principles to our pursuit of happiness. 'I either want all the happiness in the world or I want none at all'; 'If the happiness that I am getting doesn't fit into my idea of complete happiness, I let go of whatever actually comes my way' – has it begun to sound absurd just yet? A little context will do the work.

As a practice, I dedicate the last month of every year to a high spirit of reflection and planning. The very work that I do is so fulfilling in itself and so fully flowing with a myriad of experiences that it makes it a journey of joy to look back at the year gone by as well as visualising ahead for the year to come.

It was during one of these years, when I engaged in the usual process of soul-searching and introspection in December, I remember something that consistently kept echoing in my thoughts and enveloping my mind was the idea of happiness. My contemplation brought me face to face with so many situations and instances in the year gone by when I hadn't welcomed happiness because of this 'all or nothing' syndrome. On trying to connect my realisation to the people around me, I found that almost all of us were sailing in the same boat in our endeavour to either grab all the fish in the pond of happiness or let go of every bit of it.

This is how it looks from a distance: When we do not get something EXACTLY as we want it to be, we reject and overlook whatever little happiness and goodness it could be offering us in whatever form. In our attempt to want things as per the picture we have painted in our mind of 'how it should be', we are ready to lose on the little joyous experiences it can bring us by being 'how it actually is'.

I happened to realise that even when we do not get something that we wished for at all or exactly as we imagined it, we always have the choice to not be distressed about it and gain our happiness from what we may be getting instead through our struggle. After much thought, I safely came to the conclusion that there was not even one moment in my year that had gone by which was so bad or so hopeless or so out of hand that I could not have managed to stay calm in it (if not exactly happy). At the least, even in the worst of times, I felt that I had the power to avoid being sad or troubled.

I am not implying that we should be mindlessly entertaining or making peace with everything that comes our way. All I am trying to establish is that in times when things do not go as we planned them to go, the very fact that 'I TRIED MY BEST TO MAKE THEM HAPPEN IN A CERTAIN WAY' should be enough of a reason for our contentment and gratification.

The very presence of this thought in the inner discourse of my mind has made me feel happier, fuller, and more satisfied within myself which is what has strengthened my belief of practising to find goodness in everything. The very miniscule level of right in something that may not have turned out completely as expected is reason enough for us to add a happy moment in our lives.

I understand that we are not naturally groomed in such a manner but I am very sure that a conscious and continuous practice to achieve this approach or way of thinking can help us relish an absolutely delicious life full of pleasure and contentment; for there goes an ancient belief that one can be just as happy as one chooses to be.

Let us experience ALL of the happiness that is possible in our lives at any given moment and reject NOTHING of it for something else and for some time later.

Even in the worst of times, I felt that I had the power to avoid being sad or troubled.

XXIII
Embrace the Unknown

'How to become friends with our confused state of mind? How to let go of the impatient need to always reach a state of clarity?' These were the questions put up by a client friend of mine in one of our conversations.

My answer to this started with a question, which was, 'Why is it important to become friends with our confused state of mind? Or why is there a need to let go of the impatient need to always reach a state of clarity?'

And I ask these questions, because I have always believed that once the reason is known, it gets much easier to understand and process whatever comes to our mind. The how is what the doing is connected to, but the why is what emerges from our being. And there is absolutely nothing in this world which cannot be embraced once its connection with our being is established clearly.

So while I left the question open for this friend of mine, and now for everyone else who got interested in the question, I will move forward to sharing my own insights and experiences with the state of confusion and the need for clarity.

Not very long back, if someone asked me to pick one shortcoming of mine, which disturbs me the most, I would have said that I am very bad with taking suspense in my life. Though I would not call it confusion, clarity is what I always sought in everything that ever came near to me. Just for an example, if someone would just text me saying that they wish to share something with me, and will do so later, it would irk me to unimaginable levels. All my time from that text message, till I got to know what it was all about would go with heavy breaths.

And it is when I decided to take this matter to be resolved and pick this part of my personality to undergo a transformation, I realized what all was behind it. Having got to know the reasons, I understood that it all got connected to my way of being, and once that was established it automatically led to a shift in my being.

I recognized that my reason behind getting unsettled by such suspense was my anticipation of something being wrong somewhere. And because I never knew what it exactly was, it was not very difficult for my mind to assume the worst possible of what could happen and start creating thoughts about what all wrong can happen again. Yes, the word to be mindful of here is 'again'.

Reflecting on my own life, and though today I am thankful of each and everything that I have come across in this life, I could see that all the bad chapters, or the tough times that I had been through, had left their impressions on me. And I could clearly connect that not even a single mishap in my life came after knocking the door. Each time I had a difficulty staring at me, it all always sprung as a surprise. A surprise which always got converted into a shock and eventually shook a lot in my world, before it could finally settle.

'Pleasant' as a prefix to the word surprise ceased to exist for me. My subconscious mind allowed my being to get alert whenever there was an element of surprise staring at me. My being erected its defenses to keep itself safe and be prepared for whatever wrong may be in store with that surprise. Such was the impact of it that I have had sleepless nights over surprises, that eventually then turned out to be pleasant too. My strategy to avoid such times for myself, was an instant question to whoever was holding on to the surprise, 'Hoping that everything is ok?' And a 'Yes' to this could make me relax a little.

I realized that I was living in a cage, expecting a surprise to always bring something bad to me. Was this what I wanted for myself? The answer was as clear as it could get, a crystal-clear NO. And that led to this shift in my being. I allowed myself to not keep protecting myself from this. I gave myself the permission to be vulnerable. As this was the only way I could live the way I wanted. A life that embraces it all. A life that wishes to take all it can and give all it has.

For me it all got resolved, when I reflected upon my being and saw its non-alignment with my life's purpose. And that same is what I feel is the process and means for anyone who wishes to find an answer to this question for themselves. Yes, there can be many ways in 'our doing' which can help us on this path, but as I said at the very beginning, it all starts from our being, and to be able to access that core of ours is the first step and eventually will lead to all further that can be done to answer the question.

There is absolutely nothing in this world which cannot be embraced once its connection with our being is established clearly.

XXIV

Hope — Stick to It

The other day I happened to stumble upon an interview given by an actor who was talking about his life while he was in jail. Something that he said, which I could not relate to readily, made me reflect on his words further.

Amongst the many questions that he was asked, one of them revolved around what kept him going while he was serving his sentence. He was urged by the reporter to throw some light on what helped him live through those tough times and keep himself motivated.

In his response, he shared that someone had once told him to not hope for anything and it is this letting go of the hope of getting released that made him sail through the tough times.

There was a loud applause from the audience. And while I acknowledge the strength that is needed to go through such a tough experience and start all over again without being shattered, I could not resonate and connect with the idea of letting go of hope.

I, somehow, strongly believe that letting go of hope cannot be a solution for anything in life. How can hope — the one thing that we hardly ever lose, the one thing that lights our way despite darkness, the one thing that makes the impossible possible — be a hindrance to anything?

How can one not be optimistic in order to avoid being pessimistic? Something was not adding up in what he had said, and that got me to reflect deeper into it. I wondered what the missing piece of the puzzle could be.

And what came out for me was a clear understanding that it is not hope that we need to let go of. Yes, if there is anything that we can do without in such a scenario, it can be called 'expectation'. It is the expectation of something in the future that makes us see more of what is not in the present. This can have the potential of making the present look lesser, bleak, or not desired.

Sometimes our own expectations cause heartbreaks within us that even our worst enemies cannot. Frustrations engulf us due to the illusions or expectations that we impose on our reality.

One thing that I could relate to, to simplify my understanding of it, is the difference between 'hope' and 'expectation', which can be the same as the difference between ' gratitude' and 'thankfulness'.

While hope is as future-oriented as expectation, it differs from it because of the way it is accompanied by a sense of being which is at peace with what we currently have. Hope looks at the future with a sense of faith that whatever is in the present is the best place for that future to get created in the time to come.

Expectation, on the other hand, looks at the future to fulfill something which we feel we are deprived of in the present. Expectation makes the present look insufficient and inappropriate, whereas hope makes one feel at home with what is there, while being optimistic about the future at the same time.

The same is the difference between gratitude and thankfulness. While gratitude is about experiencing a state of being that is content in whatever is there for us and being grateful in anticipation, being thankful is based on being pleased only upon receiving something desirable.

Gratitude originates from a place which does not feel any void. Thankfulness, on the contrary, looks for accomplishment as the basis of acknowledgment.

To me, it made sense and helped me become grounded yet again. I hope you pick whatever is meant for you from this read and make the best possible use of this in whatever best way possible for you.

Meanwhile, I would like to leave you with this food for thought from Barack Obama:

Hope is that thing inside of us that insists, despite all the evidence to the contrary, that something better awaits us if we have the courage to reach for it and to work for it and to fight for it.

Letting go of hope cannot be a solution for anything in life.

XXV
Create the Best You

Evil! A word which generally makes us look outwards whenever it comes to mind. Something which many of us find very difficult to accept or acknowledge to be associated with our own self too. The best we usually do is to give it many mellowed down names like shortcomings or weakness or things that we can do better.

What does that actually talk about us? Does it really need to be relooked at to be better acknowledged? Well, I truly feel yes! Though there is no standard to what we can call evil, and what we should just be calling something which is not so good, understanding what is not correct to its actual intensity is very important.

I have always believed that — be it good or bad — if we do not accept it in totality with its true magnanimity, we stand a risk of not living it fully. Just like any good thing can only make us as much happy as much we celebrate it, everything which is not that good or is dangerous must also be understood in its totality to address and do necessary corrections.

We all have heard many stories about how evil prevails in the world and how it has affected society and humankind for ages. What also is common in all those tales is how the evil finally gets defeated and crushed by the good, and happiness and prosperity prevails.

Though there cannot be any question on the strength of goodness and the power it has to crush any evil of the universe, there is one important element that is mostly overlooked in all these narrations.

My understanding of all such stories, and even more my own experiences and those of people that I meet, is that what also plays a bigger role in the crushing of the devil is the ignorance or denial of the presence of evil within itself. And this holds as good for all the stories I have heard from the past, as it is for the life that goes on today.

In my profession, I am blessed enough to be able to meet people who seek help in various aspects of their lives. They all come to me because they desire to have a better life for themselves and wish to take charge to get over with their struggles. If I call it a little differently, my clients come to me with the evil that engulfs their lives and want me to help them be freed from it.

Yes, I am indeed happy to help them fight this battle and come out victorious, but generally, the war is not the one which they assumed they would be fighting while they decided to come to me. More often than not, what we end up defeating is the evil that resides within us. My role ends as soon as I can make them understand the issue in their lives, in its totality and the truest form. And it is this understanding which makes them win over it, in less time than they ever thought it would take.

Many of them eventually ask me how they could not do it all themselves earlier itself. Why did they not understand the problem like they did after meeting me? What is it that made the solution come so easily to them? And the answer in most of the situations is similar. It is the way and place we started to look at the whole issue.

The problem which we call evil was being looked at as being in someone or something other than us. And it is this one usual mistake that makes the evil look much bigger and much stronger than what it may actually be. Anything that is not in our domain is more difficult to control or manage when compared to what we have within us. The first step which is to take ownership by identifying our responsibility in the whole matter is generally the most difficult one. And it is this difficulty which makes us overlook it so easily, and try to control it from and at a place which we do not possess.

As soon as we shift the focus from outside to within, and find that source inside of us, which is evil, we become much more in control of killing the devil and come out victorious. This evil can be the ill thoughts, wrong actions or even triggered reactions. Whatever it may be, it is easiest to control when we acknowledge and understand our own responsibility in it, and thus take charge of commanding our lives.

We must always remember that acknowledging that which is NOT GOOD with us is the start of creating all that WHICH IS GOOD in our lives.

More often than not, what we end up defeating is the evil that resides within us.

XXVI
Allow the Flow

My world of life coaching gives me the privilege of witnessing and diving deep into varied human behaviour. It gives me the opportunity to see different people behaving in different ways in different situations.

What gets intriguing, though, is when an individual keeps switching from one behaviour pattern to another with a high level of frequency of change.

One thing that I have learned over the years from my life experience is that one should never feel guilty about having a frequent change in emotions, feelings, thoughts, and perceptions. I don't know for how many years now, I myself have practised honouring my momentary thoughts and feelings, and not rubbish them just because they show a deviation from what I was earlier.

However, several of my experiences with people have shown me the restlessness that they create for themselves by resisting a change that they know is happening within themselves.

The very fact that there is a departure from how they were earlier gives them enough of a reason to not have a rendezvous with the new version of themselves that they are becoming.

The denial of one's truth just because it does not look and feel familiar or the same as the previous version has made many lives remain unfulfilled. The apprehension of stepping out of the comfort zone has actually made so many lives suffocate in discomfort.

It has always surprised me to see how comfortably a lot of people deny themselves their inner truth. It is astonishing to come across the kind of reasons and excuses, and worldly arrangements that they cite to ensure that their truth does not knock at their minds and hearts.

In my understanding of the whole situation, one common factor that binds it all is the shame of not being constant. The feeling that the evolution of thoughts might get considered as instability of the mind. The perception that frequent changes in feelings and emotions are signs of a flickering mind. The tendency to confuse an expanding comfort zone with a lack of boundaries and routine.

Wow, what an irony! A life phenomenon that has the potential to bring immense fulfillment in our lives is left to stay unattended and even starve without the deserved attention.

I feel blessed to be in a position where lately I have been able to help people discover their ability to honour their truth, and the change this truth goes through as they move ahead in life.

Several of my conversations have had this realization as the basis of getting to the solutions that people are seeking. It is so rewarding to see people understand that the change that they are resisting has already happened in them. This knocking at the door is not by a guest, but by a member of that house itself. It is no outsider who is wanting to come in, but an insider who wants to make her presence felt.

This journey is sacred. Witnessing people who I partner with in their journey beginning to honour their evolving selves is ever satisfying. Seeing them not allowing anything in them to stop them from expressing their reformed thoughts and feelings is refreshing.

What makes me the happiest is when they resolve to go through any initial hiccups that they may face in the form of sarcasm and directed statements.

That moment when they realise that it is not very difficult for those who matter to us, and to whom we matter, to acknowledge and embrace our most authentic and evolving version is liberating.

That moment when they truly and deeply accept their core, their natural and most exuberant self is a moment full of honour.

I sincerely hope to be able to help this transformation happen with many more of those who get connected to me and to even those who do not, because of my belief that every fulfilled soul helps make another life accomplished.

So, the next time you find yourself feeling hesitant around the frequent changes you may be going through, remember: Progress is impossible without change. If you cannot embrace change, you can never live your live in its true essence.

It has always surprised me to see how comfortably a lot of people deny themselves their inner truth.

XXVII
Holding On or Letting Go

Life is a balance between letting go and holding on.

Let go or hold on: Who hasn't experienced a situation in their life when this dilemma has not engulfed them? Who hasn't found themselves walking on this fine line even once in life?

Now if this is a conundrum so universally faced, the question arises: How do we know when to let go and when to hold on? How do we know if we are not letting go too soon or holding on for too long?

Having personally experienced both sides of this double-edged sword, I believe that there is definitely a 'too soon' and a 'too long' when it comes to letting go and holding on. Both of these extremes do not serve the purpose as we do not give things the chance they deserve in the first case and we keep stretching things to a point beyond saturation (when absolutely nothing is left) in the second case.

I personally believe that no matter how bleak it seems, if there is a chance to make a difference by staying on, letting go should not be seen even as an option.

Irrespective of whether it is about a relationship or a task at hand, letting go — when you still could have made a difference and created something magnificent out of it — should not be given any space in our minds and hearts.

In such a scenario, all our focus must be on making things work because there is always a reason behind something that is not completely over.

Whatever we have been involved in, be it a relationship or a task, does not deserve even the thought of letting go because of the wonderfulness that it can spring up for us, having seen our best resolute self being given to it.

I am all for acknowledging the issues and challenges that crop up, but the very fact that they are seen and offer a sense of discomfort, is a sign of some work that it demands from us.

Where many of us go wrong is to overlook that it is the problem or the issue that brought the discomfort. And rather than ensuring that we work towards removing the very cause of the unease, we associate that challenge to the relationship or task itself, and thus start looking at them as the reason for our restlessness.

A pause and a resolve to address that which brought in the discomfort is what is required, rather than letting go of what is so significant for us and makes our lives beautiful.

So, when does one let go? How to know that it is not right to let go of something or someone? Yet again, the answer lies in the word itself.

We are not talking of pushing away things or people here, the words we have used are let go. And the only right time and reason to let go is for and when something or someone does not want to be there anymore.

Letting go in such situations is like opening the fist and allowing that which wants to slip away to actually slip away. Something that has already started its journey away from you and is simply being held back is best let gone, for it has no intention and will to stay on anyway.

In a nutshell, letting go should not be an option where you see that you have a chance to allow something magnificent to be created. Likewise, holding on should not be an option for something that does not exist at all. The answer to what stage with something you are in lies within. All that is needed is for the question to be asked in all sincerity and truthfulness to oneself.

I wish and hope that we all find the courage within ourselves to not let go of that which we have got for a reason, and I wish and hope that we all find the wisdom within ourselves to know of that which does not exist anymore.

A pause and a resolve to address that which brought in the discomfort is what is required.

XXVIII
Allow Vulnerability

There have been times in my life when a week begins on one note and ends on a different one. A reminder that such weeks have often given me is to be mindful of the vulnerability that we all breathe in every moment.

Vulnerability — the word itself is mostly taken as something which puts us into a zone of insecurity and unsurity. Though there is no question about the susceptibility that it places us into, it is equally a fact that this defenselessness is what opens us to the world of possibilities that we were not aware of. Multiple examples have strengthened my belief that situations become what we allow them to become for us.

As much as it is true that certain things do happen in suddenness in our life, it is also a fact that how we react to those defines what we allow them to do to us. Multiple experiences have reinforced that it works both ways. At times it is the reactions that lead to the results, and at other times it is the desired results that make us react in a certain way to specific situations.

I was pleasantly surprised to have come across someone who chose to allow herself to be immersed in situations that would bring out a certain kind of reaction in herself.

What made me feel happy about it was the fact that, being aware of what she desired for herself, she acknowledged the fact that it is only through making herself vulnerable that she can act unlike what she has been until then. The awareness about her old ways not working for her made her put herself into a place where she would act differently. Such a dare!

And being completely in sync with my belief that the universe responds when we start to work towards our fulfillment, I saw every moment becoming magical for that person. It was such a wonderful sight to see someone getting untangled with every inhale, and with every exhale releasing a knot that had tied a pure and free soul for such a long time.

And what did it all start with? That one decision to make herself vulnerable and thus, open to receive.

I do not know what may happen next, and what course her life might take in days and months to come. But what I know is whatever level of security with herself that individual will experience will have its roots in this dare to be porous when it mattered the most. The decision to allow herself to soak it all shall go a long way to not carry any unnecessary baggage that was shouldered for so long.

At times vulnerability is adopted consciously, and at times it is something that comes staring at us, making us feel unprepared for situations.

Whenever I have experienced such situations, what has helped me is to acknowledge the fact that I am not ready for it. The very acceptance that what I am encountering is not expected at all makes me accept that I am not even expected to be prepared for it. And thus, it is fine for me to not know everything about handling it all perfectly.

Such surprises do not need our perfection; instead, all they need from us is to have the right perception. What matters in situations like these is the perspective with which we look at both the situation at hand and also ourselves.

To allow us the liberty to be vulnerable when found in sudden situations helps us feel grounded, and avoid any sense of unreasonable self-created expectations from ourselves.

Every surprise turns into a situation once we give it the desired time to settle down. And once mindfully done, such situations eventually become manageable too. Having allowed myself to go through this vulnerability has helped me handle the situation at its merit, and thus sit here today feeling much more stable and peaceful.

Let us all embrace vulnerability, and permit ourselves the gift of blissful receiving that it brings with itself.

It is fine for me to not know everything about handling it all perfectly.

XXIX
The Blessing Called Vulnerability

In the world of today, I see most of the people looking for creating a safe life for themselves. The meaning and means of safety may differ, but eventually the desire is to achieve a zone where there are no uncertainties around — a life that can be lived without exposing oneself to unpredictability.

Though I myself have not been very good with taking suspense, but lately I have found myself starting to enjoy the unfamiliar. This process of making myself vulnerable has made me experience life at a level which is beyond whatever I ever imagined. This has made me come to a conclusion that vulnerability has proved to be a blessing for me and has allowed me to create magnificence in my life.

My success in being a life coach is all only because of the people who get connected to me as my clients, people who connect with me with a desire in them to know themselves better, to understand their reason of being, people who always want to create better lives for themselves. The reasons for which they seek coaching may be different but one common thing I have been blessed to have seen with everyone who benefits from coaching is for them to have the ability to allow themselves to be completely vulnerable during our coaching journey.

I know that one of the most difficult things to do when you come to a complete stranger is to bare it all and make oneself prepared to embrace it all without any filters attached. Frankly, I keep myself prepared for coming across a wall that may be there created by someone to safeguard themselves. Thankfully, I am yet to come across one.

But is the benefit of vulnerability only limited to the world of coaching? Does it not serve us to be the same way in the other areas of our life too? Well, the answer to this is simple as far as I am concerned.

My reply is based on beyond count experiences from my own life and those of others. I am of the firm belief that vulnerability is the best ingredient to include in our personality that gives us the best chance to experience life and all its beautiful offerings. It is by opening ourselves to receiving it all that we give a message out in the world of our intention to see things that only come to those who dare.

Whenever I talk about vulnerability, I am almost always asked a question about the rightfulness in putting oneself at risk. So, before I proceed, I would like to clear the air about what true vulnerability is and is not.

By advocating for vulnerability and the possibilities that it creates, I do not mean putting oneself in zones which we know are not good for us. It is and will always be foolish to try and put our hands in a boiling pan of oil and say that we were making ourselves vulnerable. The last thing that stands anywhere close to being vulnerable is being stupid. In no way, it is right to know that something is going to dis-serve us and still expose ourselves to it. That is not vulnerability. It is an open invitation to troubles and difficulties in our lives.

What vulnerability requires, though, is to unwrap ourselves of the various protective layers that we may have covered ourselves with expecting and anticipating something wrong to happen to us always. It is about dropping that shield which does not allow the fresh air to meet us and make us feel refreshed and energised. It is about uncovering ourselves from whatever we think of as being protective but is actually restrictive.

Being vulnerable is about making oneself completely ready to embrace all that life has in store for us. It is about allowing each pore in our body to accept the magnificence of life and let our soul feel fulfilled. Being vulnerable helps us drop our inhibitions and leave our prejudices about something or someone. It allows us to know people and things for what they actually are and offer rather than continuing to live in our own preconceived notions about them.

In my own life, I have experienced that I have received the most when I have allowed myself this vulnerability. And thus being open to receive, I have seen the universe respond to one's willingness to embrace it all by providing a life that offers all its various shades.

My biggest learning through all this has been that by not allowing ourselves to be vulnerable, we do not only prevent some not so good things from coming to us but also restrict the in-throw of so many wonderful things that life has to offer. And what also comes through is that a lot of these not so pleasant experiences that we are trying to avoid also eventually lead us to places that we would have not wanted to miss once we know of them.

Vulnerability is the best ingredient to include in our personality that gives us the best chance to experience life and all its beautiful offerings.

XXX
Acknowledge Appreciation

Something that has made its place in my consciousness and awareness over the last few years is how the simple act of being a humble receiver of acknowledgements that come our way makes our life, and those of others around, a life of enhanced worth.

Just like being critical is often constructed as something that can get people to push their boundaries and achieve more, giving acknowledgements to people for the good work they have done gets associated with complacency and creating flattery.

We have been told to be cautious in our appreciation of people, to not let them or lead them to become careless with things. Since the very premise on which this belief is made is wrong, the only thing that it leads to is a habit in us to be guarded in our appreciation and acknowledgement.

We do not only stop at not acknowledging people enough for what all they deserve but we also unfortunately make ourselves into individuals who start to get wary of acknowledgements even if they are directed towards us.

Now try and reflect within yourself: How do you react mostly when praises are showered upon you? What is your most natural reaction when someone speaks out all the good things about you to you? What has become your most obvious way of responding when you are appreciated and applauded for all the wonderful things that you do and for how magnificent a person you are? Yes, there may be times when you allow yourself to accept it gracefully by saying a thank you, but I have seen more than enough people who start to shrug off any such moments and start to deflect such expressions of appreciation by making it all look like not being such a big deal. Do you relate to this being you?

I am sure many of you will relate to having been this at some point in your life. And most of you may still be doing this. Have you ever reflected upon what makes us do this? And, in fact, what are we creating for the world by being like this or acting in a manner where acknowledgements are not allowed to flourish and prosper? Most of us would not have given it a thought.

What we have done is to make this habit of deflecting acknowledgements an act of displaying how humble we are. By allowing appreciation and praises to not be directed at us, we feel we have prevented ourselves from getting into a space of boastfulness. What we do not realise here is that by allowing ourselves to be individuals who deflect acknowledgements, we in fact are creating a self which is deprived of enough appreciation in life. And thus, we eventually become a source which is so depleted of acknowledgements that we find it hard to acknowledge others for what they are worth and deserve to be appreciated for.

This habit of not feeling comfortable about acknowledgements eventually is converted into a chain reaction which causes our world to be deprived of people who either feel worthy enough or can make others feel special about themselves.

On the contrary, when we ourselves become more open to receiving acknowledgements, we begin to see much more good in others than what we would if we were closed to any kind of appreciation.

Our recognition of the good in others expands to a great extent and we become magnets to even the minutest of goodness someone maybe holding in them.

A practice that can allow us to be comfortable with both receiving and giving gestures of appreciation is to bring into our life a ritual that we need to carry out twice a day. This ritual requires us to start our day by reminding ourselves about one strength of ours that we would want to use to create something beautiful during the day. We need to give ourselves a couple of minutes to acknowledge this strength of ours and appreciate our awareness of our own magnificence. We meditate and soak into the glory of all that this strength has helped us accomplish in life.

Having done this during the morning, we give ourselves another couple of minutes towards the end of the day when we reflect back on what wonderfulness we created through the day that went by and acknowledge ourselves for being an awesome soul that lived through the day!

This honest practice of acknowledging oneself and relishing one's awesomeness is so meaningful that it turns us into people who are appreciative by nature; thus, leading us to create profound possibilities in our lives!

We begin to see much more good in others than what we would if we were closed to any kind of appreciation.

Diving Within

XXXI

Bon Voyage — Taking the Trip Within

The greatest journey is the journey within.

INWARDS! A word that often preoccupies my mind. Do I get surprised by this need that keeps resurfacing? No! Is it something unusual that keeps nudging at me? Definitely no!

Every time I go through hectic schedules and am surrounded by various kinds of people for long stretches, I do so fully aware that the need for a journey within will grip my mind and thoughts with a powerful intensity pretty soon. It has become such a pattern in my life that it does not come across as something unfamiliar nor as something that makes me question its origin.

Connecting with oneself is such an important and innate aspect of life that once we become consciously aware of the value addition it makes and begin to practise it, it almost becomes addictive and as imperative as breathing in and breathing out.

My profession, which blesses me with the opportunity to interact with and understand a lot of people by getting to know their core, has made me realize that there are many misconceptions associated with the notion of 'connecting with oneself'. In my opinion, it is these misconceptions that create most of the issues for many of us today.

I meet a large number of people who seek help for various issues that bother them, and in most of the cases, the problem seems to be originating from somewhere outside of them. While presenting their case, they mostly perceive themselves as the receiver of something which is originating from an outer sphere and is creating issues with their own life.

I would be wrong if I say that I can help everyone find a solution to their problems, but I take immense satisfaction in knowing that creating the right understanding of the problem is what I have been able to achieve with almost each one of them.

The process may differ for each one of them. The path taken may not be the same. But the eventual destination, which is a better understanding of the issue they have, is almost the same for everyone.

I see the eyes sparkling at times, and many times they also get teary. And the reason behind all of that is the realization and understanding that — whatever happens outside of us, how our core reacts to it is what the occurrence finally becomes for us.

And more often than not, our reaction to what occurs outside of us is as unmindful as we are of what is inside of us. It is my strong belief that the quality of our connection with ourselves defines how we allow anything outside of us to connect with us.

To understand and handle the various aspects of our life, what we need first is to understand what we are made up of. What are the core values and the deepest thoughts that drive us in life? What is it that makes us what we are? What influences our choices and reactions?

And to get answers to all these questions, we need to create a habit of taking these journeys within. It is as important to work through the nitty-gritty of the world outside, as is to take a holiday from it all and go deep within to explore the inside universe.

Connecting and reconnecting with oneself is a blessing that we all deserve. The only important thing we need to know is that this blessing does not come from anywhere else but has to be a self-created privilege that all of us must consciously give ourselves at desired intervals.

I, for one, need this fuel of 'travelling inwards' very often, and I have a strong conviction that this is what keeps me going, and helps me to assist others in seeking help with their lives too.

Understanding and acceptance of the fact that — our awareness of what we are made up of is what leads to our ability to understand what constitutes all that which we encounter in life — makes our life a better lived one.

How our core reacts to it is what the occurrence finally becomes for us.

XXXII

Change — Let It Happen

The measure of intelligence is the ability to change.

There has never been a time in my life when I have not found myself agreeing with these words of Albert Einstein. And every now and then, experiences present themselves to strengthen my belief in what I call *change is life.*

Whether it is a caterpillar turning into a butterfly or the setting of curd or a shift and transformation that runs through the thread of humanity, changes are all around us and it wouldn't be an exaggeration to say that they are the only constants in our lives.

Thus, this word *change*,absolutely, deserves respect. More often than not, I have seen change either being resisted or being ridiculed for holding the potential of upsetting the norm. Maybe at times even creating the storm. But what it deserves is being honoured and respected for making possible what each one of us is today.

I have often wondered what makes change being greeted with so much resistance. And almost every experience of mine has made me understand and reaffirmed that the only reason why change is treated the way it is treated is because it does not always adhere to expectations.

The result that any change brings is not always what we assumed or calculated while allowing the change to happen. And it is this loss of control over the consequences or treading through the unfamiliar territories that leads us to want to control the change itself.

The work that I do blesses me with numerous experiences from a huge number of great life stories. Many of them in the recent past have added to my belief about the importance of change.

I have met people who are desperate to bring about some change in their lives but are stopped by either their self-doubts or by the inhibitions of others around them. I have seen such people feeling suffocated because they are not allowing change to create the magic that their lives deserve.

The very fact that resisting change to occur in their 'doing' world is disturbing them is proof that some change has already happened in their 'being' world.

When we move forward in this journey, it happens almost every time that these people begin to embrace their being without any inhibitions and start to feel good about the changes they have experienced within.

This helps them transition this change from their being to their doing, and eventually experience the magic that this transition brings in their lives. They begin to live a fuller and more empowered life.

Having allowed change to flow through them, they are also able to embrace the change that happens around them in others now. Having accepted change as the best thing that can happen to any life, I feel proud of seeing these people helping others understand the magnificence of allowing change to happen.

The best part about change is that we do not need to do anything special or extraordinary to create it. All that is required for us to do is not to do anything that becomes a roadblock. It is the most natural way of life and every life is able to handle its journey through all the changes.

Remember, as the saying goes, change is inevitable. Growing through it is optional. Empower yourself to be a facilitator of change rather than being resistant to it.

Being mindful of how we live is always a more meaningful way of living our life, and one question that can help us be aware of our equation with 'change', and thus help us be fulfilled individuals is:

When was the last time when I accepted change to happen both within and outside of me?

The answer to this question sows the seed for a life which flows and glows in all its magnificence.

The result that any change brings is not always what we assumed or calculated while allowing the change to happen.

XXXIII

Nothing Without Within

What a great world it is that we all have inside of us! The magical abundance and gifts of the universe that rests inside of us are protected so deep within that even we, as the beholders of it, do not get to see them unless we awaken our consciousness to this new dimension.

As a work in progress, my constant endeavour is to keep making a journey, every now and then, to this inner monastery of my existence. This journey continues each day, every day.

And with every new path travelled, it helps me become more and more aware of my magnificence and abundance. It also strengthens my belief that it is this same awesomeness which each one of us holds within us that makes this world such a beautiful place to live in.

All the wonderful achievements of humankind are a creation that originates from this wonderful core of all of us who make this our place to live and thrive in.

Thankfully, my work also gives me several opportunities to help others connect with their deeper self and thus, get familiar with the wonders that they are holding within themselves. This partnering encompasses helping others access their core and discover the natural talents and innate values with which they operate.

And though it feels like an almost impossible task to begin with for almost each one of them, most feel a sense of awakening as they gradually walk the path and discover all that which lies within.

This process of partnering is not new to me. I consider myself blessed to have held space for many souls and to have facilitated an initiation for them to connect with their core.

But, no matter how many souls I may have witnessed this for, each time the revelation of the core feels like a pious moment of ecstasy. It feels as if we are holding one's newborn version which is so tender and pure and never experienced before.

Yet each time, I have not been able to help but pay attention to how the people I participated with on this journey have not been surprised by what they found within themselves.

Not even once has there been a sense of being astonished because of disbelief. Instead, it indeed has been pleasing and also has come with a sense of stillness, as it has been the most relatable version of self that each of them has seen.

There has never been any adjustment needed for anyone to embrace who they met with the inside of them. The natural affinity and joyous acceptance have been a testimony to the fact that it has been, all along, this version of theirs that makes them complete.

All those who have been a part of this process of self-discovery with me have been living a much-fulfilled life with a sense of purpose. And this re-affirms my belief, time and again, that the human BEING has unlimited possibilities of DOING what they eventually want to.

Knowing the greater reason behind our very existence helps us align our thoughts and actions to answer our calling.

I feel blessed to be seeing these aware beings, not only create more and more success but also celebrate their success in a manner that is much more fulfilling and complete than it has ever been.

As I mentioned earlier, my journey of self-discovery continues and shall never end. It is this journey through which I feel blessed to be able to assist others to find and connect with their core-selves. It is through this journey that I see myself reaching my destinations several times in a month.

What I do is then turn every destination into a milestone and carry on further with my journey. And it is this awakening that helps me partner with so many beautiful souls in their endeavour to connect with their core.

As they say, sometimes the journey is the reward. Sometimes it is the journey that teaches us a lot about our destination.

Feel a sense of awakening as they gradually walk the path and discover all that which lies within.

XXXIV

Take Charge, March On

Changing the status-quo, sometimes, becomes the theme of life. Though different from each other in many ways, one common message that runs through all the situations in such times is to believe in oneself and take charge.

My conviction that life does not hold back what it wants you to experience has gained enough strength from such situations in life. Each of these has powered my belief that our whole life creates for itself. It has reaffirmed to me that it is in this endeavour to create that we direct our lives to how they are lived.

Two experiences come to the top of my mind when I think of such times in my life. One of these had me involved directly, and the other one was about a client of mine, who then turned into a friend, and is today creating a whole new life for himself. Being true to my intention of taking charge, I would like to mention first the one wherein I was involved.

This one particular thing that I allowed to hold me back for almost a couple of years, for no obvious reason, was brought to an end by me one fine day. It was my inhibition about a place which I had never visited but had somehow always been the reason for some kind of uneasiness whenever it became a part of any situation.

And very unlike me, I was allowing that to exist in my reality without having done something about it. This inaction of mine had allowed something outside of me to control what happens inside of me for a good twenty months or so.

But then for how long I would have been able to deny the truth of my core. And eventually, I took charge and allowed my core value of love and freedom to enable me to free myself from this and bring love to that same place which was allowed to be the reason for something exactly opposite.

Now that I look back, I understand that what I did that day was to do nothing. In fact, what I was doing before that was quite a lot of doing. Doing which was not in sync with my being. Actions that were contrary to my core, that is, love and freedom. And when I allowed myself to NOT DO anything which was not my true self, I was able to break this status quo, and that freedom allowed me to create love in the surroundings.

Surprisingly even the second situation was making its impact simultaneously. Though a lot had been happening there for a couple of weeks, it was on that very day while I was driving down to that same place, when I got on a call with someone with whom this second situation is concerned.

This client turned friend, who in his words, experienced metamorphosis shared with me a lot of things that were happening around him since he had started acknowledging his true self. Everything that he shared was so impactful and liberating that I immersed myself in the magic of life being created while enjoying the drive through the serene surroundings.

Though his talks had a lot to do about what he was doing to make all those changes come into effect, I could sense that it was only about acknowledging one's core self. It was just a change in this way of living that made all other actions so very spontaneous and easy that it all eventually led to a change in the status quo.

The sense of surprise in his words did not surprise me a bit. And it was only because I could see that it was now that life was creating itself.

Both these situations had a common factor, and that was to stop fighting with what your core is. Things may need action or inaction to change, but one thing which makes it all smooth and effortless is the acknowledgement of our true self.

An honest 'HELLO' to one's core enables our lives to say a 'GOODBYE' to all that which does not serve them. I wish more and more power to all of us to allow our lives to create for themselves what they truly deserve.

I was able to break this status quo, and that freedom allowed me to create love in the surroundings.

XXXV

Be Responsibly Response-Able

We are made wise not by the recollection of our past, but by the responsibility for our future.
~ George Bernard

Such profound meaning in what is said here. By default, responsibility must make us look forward. Though it is often mistaken as something which is past-focussed and is commonly attributed to owning what has already happened, the true sense of being responsible lies in having a vision for your future according to me.

Many times, we deflect responsibility fearing that it will bring the blame to us for something that might not have happened right in the past. At times, we are unsure of what the results may be in the future, and thus, we escape taking responsibility for doing something. And then there are times when things are not going as we expect them to be in our present, and that makes us step away from being counted as responsible for it in any way. What is common in all of the above is that somewhere we believe that things were, are, or will not be in our control, so we deny ourselves taking responsibility for it.

The truth, though, is opposite to how we look at things here. We feel no control, and thus, we shed responsibility too. But the matter of fact is that it is only when we put ourselves in a position of being responsible, we can find ourselves at a place where we can better control the situations too. The least that is assured for us is that we will have complete control over how and what we present ourselves as to whatever the situation is.

I was having an interaction with one of my clients when, all of a sudden, he asked me if he could stop talking about what he took up as the agenda for that session, and discuss something else. For me, as a coach, it is always about what and how the client wants things to go, so I did what was necessary to give things a steady pause, and then allow him the space to share what he wanted to.

The next twenty minutes that we spent together were so meaningful, and the way he went back after the completion of the session, reaffirmed my belief in the divinity of this whole coaching process. I could see that no matter what all he would have accomplished discussing everything else in his world with me, nothing would have made him feel whole unless what he talked about in those twenty minutes was what genuinely mattered to him.

There was a particular situation that he had encountered wherein, in his words, he had not taken responsibility for trying to make an impact. And because that situation did not settle most appropriately, the feeling of guilt of having not done anything about it was bothering him beyond what he ever imagined. Maintaining the ethics of my work, I cannot delve deeper into the details of the situation, but what I can surely share is the understanding that was eventually established which became the turning point for him.

Reflecting on the sequence of events, and connecting much beyond the outer layer of his perspective, he understood that having gained complete knowledge about the situation at hand, and having evaluated all the possible ways that he could respond to the situation, it was he who chose not to participate in it. It was his mindful decision to not be a part of the situation for whatever justified reasons he had for himself. It was he who opted for keeping himself away from what was happening.

IT WAS HE WHO WAS RESPONSIBLE FOR CHOOSING THAT HE WOULD NOT GET INVOLVED WITH THAT SITUATION.

And there, with this last statement, he saw the transformation in his thoughts. **Fromassuming that** just because he did not do anything about the situation, he did not take responsibility for it **tohis acceptance of the fact that** he took responsibility to not act **made him make peace with the whole thing**.

He developed an understanding that being responsible does not necessarily mean participating in everything that comes our way. The choice that we make of not being part of a situation is also how we take charge, and be responsible in a different way towards that situation.

I hope that we all develop a deeper understanding of what being responsible is, and take ownership of what we decide to do or not do, in whatever we come across during the journey of our lives.

We will have complete control over how and what we present ourselves as to whatever the situation is.

XXXVI

Present — Present It to Yourself

This was a time in my life when every situation and every conversation was full of reflections, thoughts, and projections. Though a lot was getting discussed about the past and the future, one common thing that I found missing in almost every conversation I was having with people around was the present.

And that is exactly what made me ground myself and decide to get into a zone of nothingness for maybe a day or two.

As I look at life, there is nothing more which we can live other than the present time we are breathing in. And it is this present state of mind that eventually becomes our past to reflect upon, and it is this present only which was earlier the future that we had planned for.

Nothing in this world can make me believe that the present can be compromised even if it creates the best chances of a glorious future.

Incidentally, in one of the sessions I had during this time, the same kind of thoughts were brought to the table by one of my clients. Although she was not sure as to what it is that is making her feel lost and numb, she knew that something was not the way she would have liked it to be.

This client of mine has always been an insightful and reflective person, and that is what makes her a darling for everyone around her too. We chatted for about an hour, and not once but at least on three occasions, I found her crying because she realized that something which has been her source of strength and gratefulness has suddenly turned into a cause of pain to her.

Having dug deeper into herself, and by the way the same was being done by me for myself simultaneously in the session, she discovered that both for herself as well as with others, she has allowed the present to not be lived in the process of thinking about the past and the future.

Though both of us acknowledged the power of reflection and planning, we understood that the same power can become destructive when it is not managed properly.

I knew the strength of this lady, and it came as no surprise to me that as soon as the realization presented itself to her, she spent no extra time in cribbing about it and crying over it, and straight away moved into the zone of finding solutions.

And what a simple solution she came up with: To keep forty five minutes of each day from hereon for the process of reflection and planning, and ensure that there is no further time spent allowing the present to not be fully lived.

She further segregated these forty five minutes too. She decided that she would spend fifteen minutes in the morning to go through the plan for the day so that she mindfully lives that which is about to become the present. And then, she would spend half an hour in the night before she goes off to bed to reflect on the day gone by and plan for the day yet to come.

She called me after implementing this routine for a while and when I asked her the question, "How did it go?", she corrected me and urged me to change the question to "How is it going?"

Once I did so, she replied, "It is going WONDERFUL as always."

Just as it happens almost always, each of my client's discoveries helps me live a better life too, and that is exactly what happened with this one too. It was she who discovered it for herself, but what came out was equally needed for me too at this point in my life.

If you feel that you have also been in this space in your life lately, maybe this piece of writing is not accidental for you. Maybe it was meant for you to help you make a minor adjustment and breathe in what is present now.

The present to not be lived in the process of thinking about the past and the future.

XXXVII
Self Concept

There are times in our lives when we feel overwhelmed with a sense of gratitude and blissfulness. I felt the same during one of my interactions with my life coach when something of huge relevance came up. And this was about self view.

If you are reading this today, I invite you to spend some time in the day or at least the week ahead to introspect and think about your self view.

And before this word is misunderstood, I must clarify that — by self view, I mean the unfiltered, unaffected, unadulterated view about the self that we have deep within.

I am saying deep within because all our perceptions about ourselves are protected or covered in the layers of opinions that the world has created and expressed to us about ourselves.

Having heard so many views, which are then coupled with our own judgments about us, the immediately visible self view can be very different from what we believe ourselves to be.

And that is why a pause, and a little time of introspection!

Remove yourself from the names of all the relations that you live or have ever lived.

Detach yourself from your own expectations about yourself which would have had an impact on how you perceive yourself at this moment.

Distance yourself from any judgments or opinions that you may have heard about yourself, and thus used to create notions about your self concept.

Forget about all that you have achieved in your life and even that which you have failed in.

Having shed all these layers, which initially will be difficult, think of what all forms the protective layer, or now I must call it an obstructive layer between you and your actual self. And then slowly, and gently, tear that off from yourself too.

And now that you have opened your most tender and original self to this vulnerability, see what it is that you see in yourself. Who is that person, who has revealed itself for you?

The very first look of it can be very pleasing, or very scary, but stick to it. Stick to it, because this is your true self at this very point in time and space.

And it is this true self of yours which will become the foundation of whatever your life creates from hereon.

Being aware and in total acceptance of the truth of the present moment is what will allow you to fully embrace the path that you should be taking to reach whatever you aspire for.

What you are or what you are not today is very important to be known, for you to be mindful of what all you need to be to reach where you desire to be.

What I learned from my life coach the other day is what I am going to practice right to the T. And I know that this is what is going to be my guiding torch to initiate the flame that I want to burn for spreading light to this world.

It shall remain a continuous endeavour for me from hereon, and though it might be a little difficult because of the various distractions and inhibitions, I am sure adopting this habit is going to benefit anyone who embraces this with complete sincerity.

The immediately visible self view can be very different from what we believe ourselves to be.

XXXVIII

Be Ever Evolving

This anecdote comes straight from the time of my life when I had spent months after months embarking on a journey of going deep within. Though I have always considered myself to be very aware of my own thoughts and perceptions about life, what I was experiencing during that time was something which was beyond my own comprehension.

The space inside of us is so vast that one can never know enough and all of it. Moreover, our eagerness to be kept informed about all that happens in the outside world makes it almost impossible for most to even know a bit of what their true self is.

The self-concept and self-image get created because of the comparisons with the outside world, views of the people around us, and even our own perceptions because of our reactions to what happens around us.

My experiences in my coaching work have made me witness many such instances where I have seen the kind of damage a false self-concept can do to a person. I have come across several people who are either bearing self-inflicted pains or are living in a make-belief happy world, just because of their disconnect with the reality of who they are.

My natural inclination was to go deeper into this and try and find out what brings people to this level of disconnect from their truest version.

What is it that makes people lose their sense of true self, and then helps them stay away from it? I wondered why the need to live their most authentic self does not arise in them.

The route I chose to come to any understanding of it was to go within and find out the answers that best served my ability to comprehend. And what came out when I went inside was what compelled me to stay further with this and keep exploring.

I went in with several questions, but what showed up was not an answer to any of those. Instead, what I encountered was the revelation that despite being so very well connected with my own sense of self, there was a lot more for me to explore and know about my own self.

The parts of self — which either never showed up or were pushed away by me till now, or those that I had ignored because of my own self-concept — came back running to me all at once. And it is this rendezvous which opened the floodgates, and took me into even deeper spaces within which were till now unexplored or unknown to me.

My intention here is not to reveal what all I came across but to bring to your awareness that to have a fixed self-concept is as unserving as not having a self-concept is. If people with no self-concept live a life of disconnect, having a fixed self-concept can be equally detrimental to one's continued evolution as a human being.

For anyone who lives a connected and conscious life, there will always be new experiences and new encounters happening around. And all these experiences have the power to activate something within us which may not have been a part of our mindful awareness about ourselves.

It is in situations like these that we experience ourselves having acted or reacted in a manner which was not us. Or I should say, we believe that it was not us. But the matter of fact is that there is no one else sitting inside you that can trigger any reactions. What gets activated is a part of you which was either ignored or was simply never accessed inside of you.

To go deep within, or may I say deeper within, can either be a matter of choice or a result of triggers like this. Whatever may be the reason, my experiences tell me that this continuous self-exploration helps us understand the world and people around us in a much better way. And the only reason behind this improved level of understanding is our own enhanced understanding of ourselves.

The dynamism of our self-concept is a blessing and must be used as a tool to have better connection with ourselves as well as the people and situations that we come across in our journey. I have found this to be a very interesting journey for me, and one which shall continue till I last.

Living in a make-belief happy world, just because of their disconnect with the reality of who they are.

XXXIX

Ask

I remember coming across a movie which reinforced my belief of being answerable to one's calling as our biggest obligation towards this life that we have got. It reaffirmed my notion that any life deserves to be lived true to its most authentic, most natural, most effortless form.

Becoming aware of what our true calling is and ensuring that we align our thoughts and actions to it, in order to bring harmony for ourselves as well as others around us, seems to me as our utmost responsibility. There is nothing grander than the purpose that our core nudges us and directs us towards. There is nothing more meaningful than the voice that echoes from the deepest parts that we could find within.

In my life till now, I have seen many successful yet unhappy, as well as very happy but not so successful people. By success, I mean simple material success which is measured in the form of our tangible achievements.

With most of such cases, what I have also seen with maybe an exception of only a few is for them to question their state of being. And this state of being is being questioned because of its visible non-alignment with the state of doing of these individuals.

How can one be happy if they have not created enough material success? And what makes someone who has created so much material success not be so happy in life?

From where I see, these are less of questions and more of mindset statements that are expressed in the form of questions. And it is this mindset that we need to safeguard ourselves from and make sure that we do not disconnect with our truest self, which is often reflected in how we genuinely feel, irrespective of what stage of material success we find ourselves in.

It is important to keep asking ourselves important self-accessment questions, the answers to which reveal a lot about what our core is carrying at any point in time.

I myself use these questions often, both to help my clients understand their state of being and thus find peace amongst the various outside voices which become noise at times and to keep me connected to my own self and thus be aware of why and how I feel in a certain situation.

There are many questions that enable us to go deep within and access our innermost. But what I have decided is to share with you three such questions, which you can ask yourself, and answers to which may reveal that which helps you to stay self-aware and at peace with yourself.

The most optimal condition in which to ask these questions to yourself is to be in a zone of 'NO CONDITIONS APPLY'. By that I mean, keep yourself into a complete and honest SELF-ZONE, and do not accept any answer which has anything except only and only your own self as the basis of it.

You might be playing the role of a mother, father, daughter, son, husband, wife, friend, colleague, and many more. But while you ask these questions to yourself, make sure that none of these roles play a role in either asking the question itself or answering the question that is asked.

Though this is the only prerequisite before you get into presenting yourself these questions, achieving this state of being does not come easy to most.

My advice: Do not rush into finding out the answers. Instead, start the process of practicing giving yourself that chance of experiencing yourself as what you are. It may take a few days or even a few weeks for some, but once it seems easier to practice, these questions will work wonders for you.

And because I do not want even me, as an author, to have an impact on you after having presented you with the questions, I leave you with these three questions without saying anything after them.

Three Self-Accessment Questions:

1. When do I feel happy? (*It is different from what makes me happy?*)
2. What do I seek in life? (*Do not think of it as what do I want in life?*)
3. What do I feel grateful for? (*It is not the same as what I feel happy to have?*)

The answers to which reveal a lot about what our core is carrying at any point in time.

XL

Room for Improvement

'There is always room for improvement.' I have heard this saying for years beyond my remembrance now. And though, I never actually questioned it, lately my belief in this has grown immensely because of the life experiences I have had.

Largely because of my interactions and experiences in the field of work, I have seen huge possibilities of further improvement both in myself as well as the beautiful souls I have come across.

This includes people and things whom I have seen grow in the last few years, and somehow presumed that they have reached where they were meant to be. My experiences, though, have made me realise that there is always much more still to be done or yet to be accomplished in our journey of self-growth.

This room, I mean the room for improvement, as I see it now is in fact the biggest room possible in the house of one's personality. Having embraced the idea of continued improvement, the question that naturally came to my mind was what was it that made me think otherwise about this whole thing. What was it that led me to be content with the progress I saw either in myself or in others, and thus think that there is no further possibility, or that the pinnacle has been achieved?

The answer to these questions and some more like these made me understand the issue at hand a lot better, and that is exactly what makes me share my learnings with you here.

My desire to share it with my world is based on two things, one, my endeavor to help people live fulfilling lives, and second, awareness about it may help some to reflect on themselves and those around, and thus bring the necessary improvements that are still possible to happen.

One of the things, which I realized, took my eyes away from looking at further improvement was that whatever I saw having been achieved was somewhere already beyond my earlier expectations, and thus my own standards as far as reaching satisfaction and contentment was concerned, were very low. The pleasure of having seen betterment, which fitted my own outlook, deterred me from seeking any further improvement at all, and be content with what already is.

Another reason behind this that came to the surface was that whatever improvement I was witnessing was happening at a time when subconsciously I had stopped to expect or have any hopes of anything changing for good ever. My multiple past experiences of having been disappointed must have led to such thoughts of mine, but what it also did was for me to surprise me and catch me off-guard, thus not being sure how to make any sense out of whatever good I saw happening.

The next reason, which is very true, no matter how silly it looks here, was the self-denial mode of not acknowledging the improvements that were very clearly showing up for themselves, both in people as well as myself. And this denial mode which led to not even seeing what was clearly showing itself obviously could not allow me to look for anything further or beyond.

The last but another very important reason behind this which I could identify was a fear of obsession for perfection. I understood that my belief of perfection being a place of arrogance and pride also made me think that the process of continued improvement eventually culminates at perfection. And it was my disconnect with the feelings of obsession and pride which made me distance myself from expecting or desiring continuous improvement.

All these reasons together created a situation for me which made me overlook the possibility of ever ongoing improvement. But having got this understanding, I have pledged to shift from the zone of contentment and satisfaction to a place which applauds the present level of improvement, and then encourages for the next level to be strived for.

This makes me feel much lighter, and allows me to stay afloat, being ready to acknowledge and embrace mine as well as others' improvements, while keeping a room for further improvement.

Bring the necessary improvements that are still possible to happen.

The Case of Values

XLI

Honesty – Security Precedes This Policy

Honesty! A word that has presented itself as a theme in my life time and again. There have been moments when honesty has been received as an absolute virtue and there have been moments when the same honesty has presented itself as an absolute liability — not as much to me as to those around me.

It was during one of these times in my life when I was sensing one of my own getting unusually uneasy with anyone who would be honest with them. 'What made it so?' I wondered. Automatically, I started by relooking at my understanding of honesty and what makes it a virtue in some cases and a liability in others.

Thoughts, ideas, and experiences — flashed past in the process; some from the nooks and crannies of my own life and some from those of others. And this is what came up for me:

I realised that honesty has to always begin with one's own self. While the popular opinion usually is that it is easier to fool others than to fool oneself, I feel that being dishonest with oneself is much easier than being dishonest with anyone else.

From what I understand, dishonesty to oneself does not need a cover-up. There is no need for any false narration, no need for weaving any stories. All you need to do is to shut yourself to the truth. No flowery words, no twisted facts, no manipulative moves, and no made-up situations are required. All it takes is to do absolutely nothing and just overlook the truth — behave as if it does not exist. And lo! Without any extra effort, without any extra pain, you are dishonest to yourself!

It is this effortlessness that makes dishonesty to oneself so easy, so alluring, and so frequent for a lot of us. And as practice (without doubt) makes us better in anything, we begin to master the art of being dishonest with ourselves in no time and in due course become adept at it.

Now the question arises as to what makes honesty — something that can add immense value, clarity, and transparency in our relationships — being misunderstood, and at times, taken as a liability?

My understanding of it tells me that honesty cannot be taken as a virtue only when it is served and presented to someone in whom the capacity to accept it is lacking.

Now, capacity has two parts to it. One is the appetite for the truth — the willingness, the intent to be aware of the truth. The second is the ability to digest it — the act of accepting and working with the truth gracefully.

I have realised that for honesty to not become a liability, one needs to have both the appetite and the ability to digest it.

In the name of being right or having an aspiration to be fair, one can demand to be presented with complete honesty, but unless an ability to digest is developed, it can lead to the truth being treated as a liability. Intent to hear what is honest may be there, but it has to be coupled with an ability to accept the truth and understand it in its totality without any bias or prejudice.

Honesty or truth cannot be my truth or your truth. Truth is naked, and it just needs to be seen as it is. It is not dependent on our assumptions or our understanding or our construction of it. It just is. And the most graceful thing, therefore, that we can do with it is to let it be. But how do we let it be? We let it be by acknowledging its presence in its most crude form — without any decorations, without any deviations, without any biases. We let it be by being honest about it with ourselves, no matter what the stakes and no matter what the feelings. We let it be by finding a space around it that liberates us, emancipates us!

As and when in life we develop the ability to digest the fact in its most raw form, we are sure to feel liberated. And it is this feeling of liberation that converts honesty from being a liability to become a virtue for us.

I have been practising this in my life, and though it is an ongoing process, we can all take heart from the fact that it does not wait long before it starts to shower us with its goodness. Merits of understanding, accepting, and practising honesty can clearly be visible in the way we see life and in the way life looks back at us.

The act of accepting and working with the truth gracefully.

XLII

Cherish That Which Is You!

SELF-RESPECT!

A word so commonly used yet so easily misunderstood. Or maybe not understood in its totality. And it is this difference in understanding of it that makes people handle it so differently.

Some do it perfectly, some a bit right, and others do it somewhat wrong. What I find common in all of these cases is that a little bit of dilution in its understanding, and the complete meaning of self-respect changes.

I have come across people for whom self-respect means keeping themselves in high regard. These are the kind of people who feel that thinking of themselves as always right or superior is ENOUGH. What others think or speak of them does not matter.

Thus, whenever they are ridiculed or disrespected, they cover themselves with the blanket of self-respect and create an artificial shelter to save themselves from any outside abuse.

Though it is definitely good to create a safe zone for oneself, we must remember that closing our eyes does not mean what is happening in front of us has stopped. Likewise, this self-created shelter does not protect people from being ridiculed or disrespected or abused.

What it does instead is that all the unwarranted behaviour that we had shut our eyes to increases in strength because we chose to let it remain unaddressed. And eventually, with time, it grows so big that no matter how much we try to shelter ourselves, we fail. This is because we allowed the wrong act to grow. And eventually, when we are unable to shelter ourselves, the outside influence punctures our concept of self-respect and shatters our self-belief.

Then there are these other kinds of people for whom self-respect is all about ensuring that others see them as invincible. This also implies that if they can make themselves respected by others, they feel respectful of themselves too.

This is actually the worst scenario because such people base their own self-concept on the foundation of what others think about them. Their only solace is the wishful thinking that how others look at them is actually controlled by them. Though the reality, most of the time, is totally different.

This kind of scenario is often unsustainable because of two reasons. One, you cannot always keep on controlling what others see you as. It is too much of an ask from your own self to keep on engaging in for a lifetime.

Second, those who follow your created command for a while will surely simultaneously be finding an escape route and will vanish at the first chance they get to be away from this forced appreciation business. And once either of these stop, such people find themselves staring at a self-image which is hollow and has no substance to it.

Self-respect, in actuality, is about understanding your true self. It is about knowing and appreciating your strengths as well as acknowledging what still needs to be built or improved upon within you.

And once this awareness and acceptance of oneself are achieved, it creates a dual result, which eventually converts into the true concept of self-respect. This duality lies in, one, not basing our own image upon what others think of us, and secondly not even trying to portray an image of us which must be respectful in the eyes of others.

True self-respect originates from recognizing that we are in the making. And this process will and shall continue till we last. What is important is to accept that while this process of creation and recreation goes on, we will at times find stuff which is perfectly made, and many a time will come across edges that are not well-formed.

I wish and hope that we all learn to carry both respect and self-respect on our shoulders and make the best use of these two gems that adorn our personalities.

Create an artificial shelter to save themselves from any outside abuse.

XLIII
Power — Use It Well

So wear your strongest posture now,
and see your hardest times
as more than just
the times you fell
but a range of mountains
you learned to climb.
~ Morgan Harper Nichols

Strength! A quality that each one of us wishes to possess. A quality that makes us get up and get going even when the world is crashing down. A quality that pushes us to walk a little further and run that extra mile. A quality that whispers and urges us to do the right thing.

And I strongly believe that — be it physical, mental, or the one that we associate with character — each one of us holds some form of strength, though it may vary in its intensity.

No matter what name we may choose to call these — emotional strength, mental strength, physical strength — each one is finally about what we are made of. One of these parts of our personality gets affected, and the other ones cannot remain untouched.

Think about it: How could experiencing a physical blow not test us mentally, emotionally, and character-wise? How could a dilemma or threat faced to our character not strain us physically, mentally, and emotionally. Answers to these will help you realise that we can rarely ever see any of these facets of strength in isolation.

Yes, it indeed is a blessing to understand how strong we are concerning these various aspects of our own self. But, what is also extremely critical is to know how to use these strengths during our lifetime. It is important to be consciously aware of our potency level, and not become doubtful when it comes to making the best use of our strengths.

The best use of our strengths! Yes, that is what is most important in all of this.

Some sincere introspection and an honest connection with our within definitely helps us understand what we possess. However, what it does not tell us is how to use what we hold.

I have seen and known many people who take pride in showing their strengths. In fact, they look for opportunities where they can display their basket of beautifully decorated strengths that they either got through inherited genes, or they actually worked hard to practice and acquire.

The irony, though, is that I have also seen the very same people not being able to use those same very strengths when it is actually needed. These are the times when they face some challenges in life, and life presents them with a chance to make the best use of their strengths to come out victorious. Sadly, a huge number fails when it is most needed.

That creates this thought of what is the best use of our strengths. What do we do with these gems in our personality? Do we just use them as a piece that helps us glorify ourselves for audience displays?

The reply most obviously is 'NO'. Our strengths are not meant to be used for public display or to polish our egos. We are blessed with them so that they can be utilized when we actually need them in life. They are supposed to be put into use when the challenges of life are out there, wanting to test what we are made up of.

Strengths are not meant to be used as swords but are best honoured when we use them as shields to protect ourselves in the times of adversity.

Our strengths should not make us someone who creates wars. They should instead turn us into warriors, who are able to defend ourselves against every attack, to not be defeated and thus emerge as winners.

It is a good habit for all of us to reflect and understand what strengths we hold in our personality. And once we become aware of these gems, we must introspect with complete honesty to understand how we use them in our lives.

Look for opportunities where they can display their basket of beautifully decorated strengths

XLIV

The True Strength of Forgiveness

Mahatma Gandhi said: *The weak can never forgive. Forgiveness is the attribute of the strong.*

So many of us agree with this statement. Yet, so many of us struggle to understand it to the letter and grapple to practise it in our lives in its entirety.

The statement that Gandhi made has two crucial words in it that need to be grasped deeply and looked at with absolute contemplation to be able to fully and rightly understand the essence of this idea of his.

And these words are: *forgiveness* and *strong*.

Forgiveness — What a beautiful word! As soon as we think of this word in our heart, a feeling of connecting to a higher self emerges within. Most times, the imagery that this word creates is that of us being able to let go of and release a negative emotion such as anger, hatred, or disappointment towards the other.

The reasons for these negative emotions could be many. It could be our unpleasant experiences with some people or the wrongdoings inflicted upon us by life or our trust being broken. All of these lead us to host some extremely unserving emotions or feelings towards others.

On the face of it, these unserving emotions or feelings are being directed towards someone else. This signifies that our anger, our hatred, our disappointment are felt and meant for someone else.

While this may be somewhat true, there is another side to this coin that needs to be paid attention to.

Unfortunately, the other side often gets overlooked. However, it is the side that helps us understand the meaning of forgiveness in its true form. This side is: Even though someone else is the target of our negative, unserving emotions, we are the beholders of them — before, during, and even after they have been aimed at others.

And what does this suggest? This simple truth shows us that when our negative emotion starts from us much before it is directed towards someone else, how can our forgiveness be only driven and directed towards others. How will it not originate and begin with us?

Therefore — in order to justify the meaning of the word *forgiveness* — even before we think of forgiving someone else for the wrong they might have done to us, we need to begin with forgiving ourselves for holding a grudge that did not allow us to be our truest selves.

We did no less damage to ourselves by being angry, or disappointed, or hosting hatred than what others might have inflicted upon us. As a matter of fact, our own wrongdoing was much worse because it originated from a zone of ignorance, and thus, the ill effects also went unnoticed without any damage control.

And then there comes the word *strong*. My own understanding about this is a little different than what is generally construed as a definition of strength.

On the face of it, it seems that to forgive is a symbol of strength because it takes courage to let go of our resentment or bitterness for someone due to what we perceive was done by them to us.

My perspective on this is that the strength in question is not really in the act of letting go. In fact, it lies in acknowledging that by allowing ourselves to host negativity because of someone else's actions, the most wrong that was done to us was by us.

The general tendency is to take pride in letting go and not taking revenge for the wrong done to us. But what we also need to acknowledge (and for me that is what takes real strength) is that what we are letting go of is something that did not allow us to operate from our highest version.

This strength that we display by the way of this acknowledgement helps us make a wise call of being mindful before we allow something alike to impact us ever again. And according to me, that is where true strength lies.

Forgiving ourselves for holding a grudge that did not allow us to be our truest selves.

XLV

Give Yourself Wings to Fly

In a time of deceit, telling the truth is a revolutionary act.
~ George Orwell

I am yet to find a person whose life has not been influenced, directly or indirectly, by the word truth. I am yet to find a person who does not hope to be served with truth by others. However, despite this shared need of receiving truth, I have also, unfortunately, seen this word being misused and mishandled for no reasons whatsoever.

With all the expansive experiences that life has blessed me with, if there is one thing that I can say for sure, it is that no reason is ever valid enough for compromising on truth.

And I say this, especially after having lived a journey, where even I have tried to take refuge in the concealment of the truth, by citing various validations to myself and others.

But having left that thing in the past, I am glad that I do not find any merit in giving lies any space in my life anymore.

If I now encounter those tangents in life where I find myself in a difficult spot to honour truth, I prefer to move away from such a space rather than providing fodder for untruth to breed and thrive.

Anything or anyone, which can lead me to feel that taking refuge behind untruth is alright, does not find my company once I become aware of its intent or capacity.

Being truthful and not allowing oneself to be manipulated by reasons of why one chose to take help of a lie is a place which we all must strive for ourselves to reach.

The life we have got has a much grander purpose than the simple acts of breathing, eating, and working to create a living. No matter how high we climb on the ladder of success, it will never be an elevated life if we fail to present ourselves with a space which allows us to be completely honest.

Having had these thoughts about truth surrounding me for quite a while in my life now, one question that engulfed my mind was the association between untruthfulness and low self-esteem.

Every iota of thought and mindfulness that I could give to dig the answer to this inquiry of mine from within brought me to just one conclusion: The basic foundation on anything that is not truth lies in our reduced image of our own self.

There is no situation and no individual that is big enough for us to feel small and compromise our integrity. Instead, what we do is to reduce ourselves to a smaller size and a weaker version of ourselves that finds all suitable justifications to cling on to reasons to lie or hide the truth.

This journey to have nothing but the truth that surrounds your life starts with the toughest first step. And though we are outstanding creators of reasons as to why we could not speak the truth to others, what we need to do first is to identify and thrash all and any justifications that we give to us for not being truthful to ourselves.

This first step of being completely honest with oneself about oneself is the first, the most difficult, and the most time-consuming in our journey to the freedom that truthfulness holds. And do we need to, or actually want to take this journey forward or not, is what we can decide once we cover the first step.

Not all lives decide to take up this path to liberation. But for those who aspire and resolve to fight it out, all I wish to say is that every failure you meet on this path is success in itself.

I leave you with this thought that I read somewhere:

In the long run, the most unpleasant truth is a safer companion than a pleasant falsehood.

So, choose truth — if not for your comfort, then for your liberation!

I am glad that I do not find any merit in giving lies any space in my life anymore.

XLVI

Discipline

You must have had times in your life when your calendar suddenly gets swarmed with a lot of unplanned activities. Everything needs your attention all at once but without giving you any advance notice. It is as though the world will stop in the absence of your action. It is as though the Earth revolves not on an imaginary orbit and rotates not on an imaginary axis, but on your shoulders.

And it is in times such as these that the one thing which is needed the most has the potential to be ignored the most too. I am talking about discipline.

Discipline — the bridge between our goals and accomplishments; discipline — the enabler that helps us establish our power over our habits, routines, and priorities instead of being under their command; that same discipline gets sidelined and disregarded. We turn a blind eye to the same discipline.

Discipline is one aspect of my life which I have always been happy about with myself for a long-long time now. But what I have experienced sometimes is that despite wanting to be disciplined with a lot of things, we somehow allow ourselves to not be disciplined in some situations.

So, I am choosing this space as much of a reminder and reinforcement to myself as it is for anyone who reads it and can take whatever makes sense to them in what I share.

The role that discipline plays to keep our lives meaningful and mindful, and the experiences I have had having lived both a life with and without discipline, is what strengthens my belief about its importance in our life.

I have always believed that discipline must eventually become our natural way of being, even if in its early stages it is something which we practice consciously to adopt as a habit in our life. It should become as effortless and intuitive to us as taking the next breath or the blinking of our eyes.

My reason behind saying that it must come naturally to us is that anything which is continued to be superficially present in our life leaves sooner or later. And even till the time it stays, it does not impact our lives as much as it could naturally have.

My very own experience with discipline or I should say the lack of discipline is that there are a few factors which always make their presence felt whenever indiscipline shows up in our life.

The top three which I would like to share are: prioritizing fun above passion, not being mindful of how we are spending our time, and last but very important, not holding ourselves accountable.

When I talk of fun, I am pointing towards meaningless fun. Meaningless in the form of being directionless, or being overdone, or being done just for the sake of it. While practicing one's passion can be a huge source of fun, indiscipline generally takes us to forms of fun which we do not connect naturally to us.

Time consciousness is something which suffers the most as soon as indiscipline knocks at our doors. We start to borrow time from things which need our attention and give it to those which do not contribute to our development or mindful living in any way.

Lastly, our self-accountability takes a huge hit, for us to allow ourselves to be away from discipline. We either do not realize that we are hanging on indiscipline in how we are being, or to make things even worse, when this truth shows up on itself, we do whatever it takes to deflect it away and live in a make-believe world that all is well.

A genuine practice of self-reflection, and in case if traces of any of these three is found — taking charge of oneself, and practicing self-honesty, is what can take care not only of these three, but also many more such reasons which can allow us to make space for indiscipline in our lives.

In times such as these, I always consciously decide to pull myself up and allow my most natural disciplined self to take charge. And I hope that anyone who reads this and finds any resonance with it will try and introspect to locate any such traces, and subsequently will correct them for good.

Indiscipline generally takes us to forms of fun which we do not connect naturally to us.

XLVII

Rebuilding Trust — Authenticity

At some point or the other in our lives, we may have found ourselves grappling with the idea and feeling of trust. There might have been times in our lives when our trust would have been dented or broken. It is what to do in such situations that I want to talk about now.

When I choose the word dented and broken, I am very mindful of not picking lost as the word to mention while talking about trust. My own personal opinion and thought about it is that for trust to be lost completely, it takes a lot. And there is never a loss of trust before the signs of it being dented or broken become visible.

Therefore, in this as well as the subsequent chapters, I want to touch upon four critical things to be kept in mind or four critical ways in which trust, once dented, can be repaired and can be regained to live the blessing that this life is. I call these ways the ABCD of rebuilding trust. And, the A in that stands for Authenticity.

One thing that for sure finds its place in a space where trust suffers is for genuineness to stop existing. This lack of genuineness can be about the person in question; it can be about the talks; it can be also about thoughts and feelings; it can be about the facts being twisted and presented wrongly; and many more similar things. One word which is the exact opposite of this lack of genuineness is authenticity.

My firm belief is that, if there is an honest intent to rebuild trust because we understand the blessing that a person or a situation or in fact a thing brings to us, authenticity is one thing and the first thing that we need to commit to for ourselves. We need to make a commitment that, despite the circumstances, authenticity will exist in each and every thing that will be lived, shared, and experienced going forward.

Authenticity does not mean being in a good-looking space; authenticity does not mean speaking and doing things that please people; authenticity does not mean changing one's self only because someone else wants it that way. I am not saying that allowing a change for good in you is wrong. But if that comes from a source of authenticity or not is something which can be very easily accessed if you look within.

And this looking within also needs to be a hundred percent authentic. The people who are dear to us, the things that are important to us, the situations that matter to us, they all deserve to have our most authentic and honest self. Anything and absolutely everything which is done, even if it is done with an intent of not creating unpleasantness, that lacks authenticity is not what is deserved by both ourselves and by those who are connected to us.

The commitment must be to ensure that authenticity will exist, no matter what. And if there is any work to be done, it would be done on that authenticity to be understood and received well.

My personal experience in both my personal relationships and my coaching associations have strengthened my belief that authenticity creates understanding. This understanding may or may not lead to agreement and acceptance, but it will for sure lead to harmony, both within ourselves and for those who matter to us.

Once the acknowledgement of the trust having dented or broken is established, it takes courage to acknowledge that love is struggling. It takes courage to acknowledge that things are not how they are supposed to be. But this very expression of acknowledging and speaking out is the first step that we take towards authenticity.

It is understandable that things are not going to be all pleasant and joyous when this journey starts. There is going to be pain and doubt, and there is going to be some impact of what has been lived in the past. But it is this intent of being authentic to oneself and those around that will eventually lead us to a space wherein the pain will start to heal, doubts will start to fade away, and the effect of the past will begin to disappear.

Yes, there will be times when you will fall back into the pattern of not being completely authentic. There will be times when you will not find yourself strong enough to speak the truth. The only thing to be remembered during such times is the cost of it all. Having experienced the cracks or the dents and having seen that it damages our most cherished people, there is no doubt in my mind that we will find our motivation in authenticity.

Authenticity is one thing and the first thing that we need to commit to for ourselves.

XLVIII

Rebuilding Trust — Beyondness

The word beyond, as far as rebuilding trust is concerned, stays true to its actual meaning. There is no doubt that trust once broken leaves its injury marks, bitter memories, doubts that still haunt and the moments of weakness which can allow us to be or to do things which may not be the reflection of our most authentic self.

Irony is that we try to rebuild trust while being surrounded by all these unserving and unhealthy emotions and thoughts which do no good to the cause of trust being built upon again. That is where the word beyond comes into play in its truest sense.

If at all we need to give a chance for trust to be rebuilt, one of the most critical decisions we will have to take is to move beyond the negative feelings of doubt, apprehension, bitterness and living in the past using past experiences as a reference point for whatever happens in our present.

Living beyond has to be initially a conscious choice because we are acknowledging intention to make a shift from one state of thinking to another state. We need to understand and accept that the natural tendency of our past experiences is to come back again and again and haunt us.

The reason that such experiences would not die on their own volition is that they have found a good host in us giving them enough attention and importance.

We generally find it difficult to put behind our past experiences which lead to the trust being broken or damaged because it creates a sense of insecurity in us that the same might get repeated. The question here is that if the act of mistrust originated from someone else, how can our keeping it in our mind and not moving beyond it will make someone else not repeat the same?

Another act of rebuilding trust is to look beyond the act of mistrust or hurt, and look at the reasons behind trust having been broken. Though nothing can justify an act of betrayal, looking towards the reasons behind it can serve us in a dual manner. One, it can help us come out of the mode of sulking. Two, it may make us understand if we have been responsible in any way towards causing trust to be broken.

In both these cases the focus shifts to oneself, and thus we provide ourselves the best chance to be a contributor to rebuilding trust with those who matter to us.This space of self-reflection also allows us to not hide behind reasons, and justify our act of betrayal. It enables us to move beyond whatever made us let go of our most authentic self and become someone who is the creator of mistrust and hurt for our fellow beings.

Another important dimension of going beyond is to start looking beyond our expectations and perceptions of a future based on trust and faith.

This enables us to embrace and allow ourselves to be vulnerable and thus enjoy to the maximum whatever greatness the future holds for a more truthful and faithful version of ours. I am choosing to use the word faithful consciously, because this is another example of moving beyond. In this case, it is about moving beyond the practice of trusting.

Faith, which is a level beyond, is about being ready to embrace whatever comes our way, with a feeling of gratitude and a sense of calmness. This practice of bringing in faith in our life helps us gain the necessary strength to move beyond our understanding of anything which may not have happened as we would have wanted it to. It takes us beyond the measuring parameters of trust, and allows us to believe in the goodness of the universe and receive fully whatever it wants us to come across in our journey of rebuilding trust.

One final possibility that is connected to all of this is to look beyond our own understanding of what truth is. Truth exists in three forms, my truth, your truth and the actual truth. And it is the truth which exists in either our or someone else's mind which must be relooked upon for its validity at times.

A commitment towards being authentic, coupled with the readiness to look beyond, is a great enabler of rebuilding broken trust. I believe that it all starts with an intention to save and savor the relationships with people who matter to us, and there is nothing stronger that exists, other than an honest intention, which makes the seemingly impossible possible.

Move beyond whatever made us let go of our most authentic self.

XLIX

Rebuilding Trust — Compassion

According to me, something that is absolutely critical and important in rebuilding trust that is broken and dented is compassion. This ten letter word is as effective and meaningful in rebuilding trust as it is in making up of the wonderful possibility that we all are.

And though authenticity and beyondness are two practices which may need a conscious effort, compassion because of the element of passion hidden in it becomes one of the most joy-giving steps in the process of rebuilding trust.

I believe that nothing is impossible. Yet, I know somehow that it is very difficult to make someone practise compassion by preaching it to them. While I acknowledge this difficulty, I must also say that being compassionate is one of the most natural and instinctive qualities of a human being. Some things which get connected with broken trust are ill-feelings like hurt, anger, disappointment, and rebelliousness. And all these feelings, more often than not, get expressed only after having been suppressed for a relatively longer duration of time.

And here, I would like to share one of the strongest beliefs that I have had in my life and which has proven itself to be true at more than many occasions throughout my life. This belief is that anything which is suppressed reveals itself eventually with a blast. And this blast is loud! And this blast creates a lot of destruction whenever and wherever it happens!

To counter such huge reactions, one needs to have an equally strong passion to take care of the situation without giving up. And it is this passion which is hidden in the word compassion but must take charge in order to heal that which hurts when there is damage caused by the trust that has been deceived.

Compassion allows us to understand and accept the reactions of the person who is at the receiving end of the broken trust. Being compassionate enables us to hold the space for strong reactions and to let all that which is suppressed to be released in whatever best way it can be. Being compassionate helps us not wear the defensive or the reasoning hat and thus dilute the process of rebuilding trust.

The process of rebuilding trust is equally important and as hard for the person who because of having surrendered to the circumstances allowed himself to be the creator of the cracks. The very fact that this person is showing an intent of rebuilding trust is a testimony of the realisation of having been wrong.

Compassion must be shown towards this act of courage of accepting one's shortcomings. It is only this act of being compassionate that can motivate and propel a person to move forward on this path of recovery and repair. We must understand and acknowledge that the feelings of uncertainty, guilt, and self hatred are quite normal to be surrounding such a person. And the biggest support that can be given to someone who is intending to walk the path of correction is to practise compassion towards him or her.

Another aspect when we talk about compassion is to practise compassion for oneself. No matter which side of the broken trust you are at, there is either a feeling of hurt or a feeling of guilt that makes its presence felt; and there is no better medicine than being compassionate to heal the wounds that such strong feelings of hurt and guilt can inflict.

We must be compassionate towards ourselves and acknowledge our strength and intention towards rebuilding broken trust. Despite being the receiver or creator of dented trust, the very fact that we have chosen to be a part of this process deserves for us to be loving and compassionate towards ourselves.

Another very critical aspect in this process is not to be doubtful of the things which have actually never been shadowed by any kind of mistrust ever. It is quite natural for us to start doubting or questioning everything that ever existed. It is in these times that we start to question the validity and truthfulness even of that which never had a shadow of doubt earlier.

Compassion allows us to keep all that which is clean, loving, and true to be separated and cherished without raising a question while you answer all that is required to be answered during this process of rebuilding trust.

Compassionate enables us to hold the space for strong reactions.

L

Rebuilding Trust — Directness

Directness is something which holds a great significance in the kind of communication that should happen when two people find themselves in a situation that lacks trust. Patience is one thing which makes its way out as soon as lack of trust becomes visible. And thus, it is only natural for the person who is at the receiving end of the betrayal to find it hard to listen to the excuses and justifications of the person who was the creator of broken trust.

Even the person who has been the creator of the broken trust tries to find every opportunity possible to hide the feeling of guilt or shame behind reasoning and justifications. The way I look at it is that the very fact that there are two people trying and struggling means that there is an intention to change course and to correct whatever has been allowed to go wrong.

Irony is that while one person wants to take the route of justification and explanation, the unfortunate experience of the other one does not allow her to believe what is spoken even if it comes from a place of truth.

In such a scenario, being direct is something which helps immensely to rebuild the trust which has been affected. Rebuilding trust is a slow and steady process and one thing which supports it the most is for clarity and confidence to be visible without any filtration. Being direct in our communication and actions helps anyone and everyone who is somehow involved in either being wrong or being wronged come face to face with the true intentions as fast as possible.

Conversations cannot be guaranteed to be pleasant and understanding for a longer duration when a person is hurt because of being betrayed or is in guilt because of having betrayed. Being direct provides the best chance to allow the message to be delivered and received even while this space of unsurety exists. It definitely allows a better chance for understanding and confidence to regain their place between people who have been a party to this space of broken trust.

It takes courage to be direct but it is this courage which also reflects the strong intention and willingness of a person to course correct and be rightful. This courage also acts as a source of strength to the person who is hurt but is still wanting to see a ray of hope to move into the zone of believing and trusting, once again.

Be strong, be direct, and once things go to the zone of being pleasant and much stronger, you can always have as much time as you want for yourself to give and receive explanations in order to be complete with that situation of broken trust.

To summarise, the ABCD of rebuilding trust are authenticity, beyondness, compassion, and directness.

By authenticity, I mean a desire and intention to be totally authentic in whatever is being spoken, felt, expressed or experienced. A promise to be authentic goes a long way in rebuilding trust.

The practice of beyondness is about looking beyond the very act of the trust being dented to focusing on the various reasons that could have contributed from both the sides in reaching that state where trust was impacted. Looking beyond helps us be more receptive to the idea of rebuilding trust.

The third pillar is compassion which is one of the most natural ways of being for anyone. It is a very strong tool which provides love, care, and necessary support to the one who is hurt as well as to the one who is experiencing this feeling of guilt and shame because of having broken the trust.

Lastly, directness helps us present as well as receive the intention without it having been clouded under explanations and reasonings which may be hard to receive as well as present in that vulnerable state of being as a party to the broken trust.

Allows a better chance for understanding and confidence to regain their place

In Gratitude

Out of the most exquisite, the most precious treasures we can offer someone — the one thing that tops for me and becomes irreplaceable is time.

It is for that time which you have spent going through the book that I want to sincerely thank you. A deeply felt gratitude for engaging with my inner world presented to you in the form of Experiences Expressed, and for hopefully transcending it to alter experiences in your inner world!

Irrespective of whether you found meaning in the ideas that I shared or revamped them to suit your needs and life, I am glad that we could become a part of each other's world and journey.

I hope that the ideas shared in this book will help you in your life and expand themselves through your life-affirming, powerful manifestations.

If Experiences Expressed nudged you towards experiences that you would like me to know, I would be happy to connect with you. Feel free to write at connect@saiwithcoachrb.com.

May peace be upon you!